The
FORD TIMES
COOKBOOK

Favorite Recipes from
Popular American Restaurants

Recipes compiled and tested by

NANCY KENNEDY

Women's Editor, *Ford Times*

SIMON AND SCHUSTER   NEW YORK

FOREWORD

This volume is the fifth in a series of cookbooks based on the popular *Ford Times* feature which each month presents favorite recipes from selected restaurants in all parts of the country. Former editions were published under the title *Ford Treasury of Favorite Recipes from Famous Eating Places.* Now the name has been changed — we have decided to call it what everyone has always called it: *The Ford Times Cookbook* — but you will find the contents as intriguing, informative and useful as ever.

As with previous volumes, the new *Ford Times Cookbook* is intended to serve not only as a collection of recipes for the adventurous home chef, but also as a guide to good eating for the explorer on America's highways.

When *Ford Times* inaugurated its "Favorite Recipes" section over twenty years ago, car owners were just beginning to rediscover the pleasures of travel on the American road after the restrictions of wartime. As the years have passed, the average motorist has become much more sophisticated, and today he is highly selective in his choice of itinerary, resorts and eating places.

Yet, one pleasure is never dulled — that of discovering a friendly inn that offers hospitality, good service and an excellent meal. It may be a steakhouse in a small western town or an elegant metropolitan restaurant noted for its continental cuisine. Each in its own way can be a delight.

As in the past, this is a completely new collection of favorite recipes. But with this edition a special feature has been added — a selection of all-time favorite recipes taken from the preceding four volumes, all of which are now out of print. These are the recipes that our readers most prized and mentioned most often, and we are sharing them with you again. We wish you good eating and happy motoring!

CONTENTS

Contents

7

Contents

Contents   9

Connecticut

Maine

Massachusetts

New Hampshire

New Jersey

New York

Pennsylvania

Rhode Island

Vermont

Ontario

Quebec

This is a land abounding in culinary riches with food traditions that go back to the earliest days of the United States and Canada. Many recipes go back even further, brought here by colonial settlers from the Old World and adapted to the delectable foods they found in this region. Today the gourmet may spend endless days exploring the historic country inns or a lifetime sampling the countless fine eating places in New York, Montreal, and other metropolitan areas.

Painting by Paul Decker

NORTHEAST

The Prime Steer Restaurant, Norwich

Beef is the specialty of this establishment; however, the desserts and seafood dishes are equally famous. On State Highway 32 in Norwich (543 West Thames Street), it can be reached by taking Exit 80 from the Connecticut Turnpike, then proceeding east on Route 82 to traffic light and left on Route 32. Open every day for lunch and dinner from 11:00 A.M. to 10:00 P.M. Reservations advisable on weekends. Closed only on Christmas Day. Painting by Howard Connolly.

Tenderloin of Beef en Casserole
1½ pounds sliced tenderloin
1   large onion, minced
¼   cup butter
1   clove garlic, minced
¼   teaspoon oregano
1   teaspoon good beef base
    or bouillon cube
¼   teaspoon monosodium
    glutamate
½   teaspoon salt
¼   teaspoon freshly ground
    pepper
1   teaspoon freshly chopped
    parsley
¼   cup fresh or canned
    mushrooms
½   cup red Burgundy

Sauté minced onion in butter until amber, add tenderloin and mushrooms and all spices including parsley. When beef is done as desired (5 minutes for rare, 7 for medium, over high flame), add Burgundy and cook for 1 minute more. Serve in casserole. Serves 4.

The Old Well, Simsbury

The German love of good food and pleasant *freundlich* atmosphere are prominent attributes of the Old Well, located on Tarifville Road, near Route 10. Open from noon till 1:00 A.M. weekdays, Sundays till 9:00, the Old Well offers novel "extras" such as a children's menu attached to a child's storybook. Closed Tuesdays, Christmas Day, and the first week in August. Reservations suggested. Painting by Richard Langseth-Christensen.

Kassler Rippchen

Cook 6 pounds smoked loin of pork (have butcher crack bone) in boiling water for 1 hour. Remove skin. Place in baking pan in hot oven (425°) for 15 minutes. Baste with 1 cup fruit juice (pineapple and cherry), 1 cup sherry. Dredge with 1 cup brown sugar. Lower heat to 350° and bake 25 minutes more, until glazed and shiny. Serve on platter with sauerkraut and potato dumplings. Serves 6–8.

Mermaid Tavern, Stratford

This fine restaurant, which is a part of the Stratford Motor Inn, is a replica of London's famous 17th Century Inn where William Shakespeare and his contemporaries dined. Open every day, the Tavern features a Hunt Breakfast until 11:00 A.M., lunch until 2:30 P.M., and dinner from 5:30 to 10:00 P.M. Overnight accommodations and recreation facilities available at the Inn. About an hour and a quarter's drive from New York City, it is reached from Merritt Parkway by taking Exit 53N and circling around to the Inn, which is high on a hill. From the Connecticut Turnpike, take Exit 32, right one block to Main Street (Route 110), then left off Main Street for about four miles to the Inn. Reservations suggested. Painting by John Austin.

Roast Native Duckling with Honey-Mint Sauce

Season a 3-4-pound duck with onion, celery, pinch of rosemary, salt and pepper. Roast duckling in oven at 450° to 475° for about 1½ hours. Drain off grease after first 40 minutes. Serve duck with Honey-Mint Sauce and Wild Rice and Date Stuffing. Serves 4.

Sauce

Bring 1 cup honey and ¼ cup vinegar to boil, let simmer for 10 minutes. Add 1 teaspoon cornstarch which has been mixed with a little water, bring back to boil. Add 1 ounce whiskey, juice of 1 lemon and ¼ cup fresh chopped mint (or dissolve 2 tablespoons dried mint in small amount of vinegar).

Wild Rice and Date Stuffing

Put 2 teaspoons butter in a small pot and add ¼ cup chopped onion. Sauté slowly for 3-4 minutes. Add 1 cup wild rice, 1¾ cups water, ¾ teaspoon salt and bay leaf. Bring to boil. Cover and place in oven for 35 minutes at 350°. Remove from oven, add a handful of chopped dates.

Cobb's Mill Inn, Weston

A picturesque mill which dates back to pre-Revolutionary days was converted to house this delightful restaurant. Take Exit 42 from the Merritt Parkway, then travel 4¼ miles north on Connecticut Route 57. From Connecticut Thruway, take Exits 17-18 pick up Connecticut 57 in center of Westport and proceed north for seven miles. Lunch and dinner served every day except Christmas. Reservations advisable. Painting by Alois Fabry.

Ham and Cauliflower Casserole

1	large head cauliflower
1½	cups diced, cooked ham
¼	cup butter
3	tablespoons chopped chives or green onions
1	cup sour cream
½	teaspoon paprika
¼	teaspoon salt
	dash white pepper
	dash nutmeg
2	egg yolks, beaten lightly
⅓	cup grated sharp Cheddar cheese

Cook cauliflower in salted water until almost done. Drain, cool enough to handle and break into flowerets. Grease casserole and make alternate layers of cauliflower and ham. Dot with butter. Mix remaining ingredients except for cheese. Pour into casserole. Bake, covered, in moderate oven (375°) until bubbly, about 30 minutes. Remove cover, top with layer of cheese and bake until browned, about 15 minutes, or put under broiler to brown. Serves 6.

Fisherman's Wharf Inn and Motel, Boothbay Harbor

A haven for travelers, extending 195 feet into picturesque Boothbay Harbor, the Inn offers an unsurpassed view of the bustling activity of the harbor from the dining room or guest rooms. Breakfast, lunch, and dinner served daily from 11:30 A.M. to 9:30 P.M.; Sunday, noon to 8:30 P.M. Overnight accommodations and vacation facilities. Open May 27 to October 24. The address is 42 Commercial Street. Painting by F. Wenderoth Saunders.

Baked Lobster

Split and clean a live lobster for each serving. Hold claws of lobster in left hand. Place lobster on its back, insert a sharp stiff-bladed knife between where the claws join, and split toward tail (be careful to split through upper shell only). Pull plugs from claws, but do not crack claws as this lets juices out. Remove craw and intestinal tract (it leads from craw to end of tail); rinse cavity with fresh water under faucet — be careful not to remove tomalley or liver. Sprinkle cavity with salt and cracker crumbs, coarsely ground, and pour melted butter on crumbs until moistened.

Bake in 450° oven until end of tail is crisp (about 30 minutes). Serve hot with melted butter for dipping.

Baked Scallops

Place 1½-2 pounds scallops in shallow earthenware pan, in lemon butter (¼ pound melted butter with juice of ½ lemon), enough to cover bottom quite generously (¼ inch). Roll scallops in the lemon butter; then make sure they are flat in the pan. Sprinkle with salt, pepper, and cracker crumbs. Cook in 400° oven for 25-30 minutes and serve hot. (Or broil in preheated broiler, 6 inches from flame, for 20 minutes.) Serves 4.

Kennebago Lake Club, Kennebago Lake

Surrounded by 100 square miles of mountains, lakes and woods, this rustic resort owned by Bud Russell offers a wide variety of vacation activities, combined with excellent food. Open for breakfast, lunch and dinner every day; overnight accommodations. Reservations advisable for meals as well as rooms or cabins. In the western part of the state, near the Canadian border, it is 10 miles north of Rangeley. Painting by Richard Kranz.

Salt Pork Apple Pie

6 large tart apples, peeled and sliced
2 ¼-inch slices of fat salt pork, diced
1 cup sugar
pinch of cinnamon and nutmeg
1-2 teaspoons lemon juice
pie pastry for two 9-inch crusts

Fry pork slowly until golden brown — don't burn! Line 1½-inch-deep pie plate with pastry and cover with apple slices. Mix sugar and spices and sprinkle over apples. Drip lemon juice over apples. Pour salt pork with its fat over filling. Cover with top crust and prick it. Bake 10 minutes in 425° oven; then in 350° oven for 30 minutes.

Maple Nut Tapioca Pudding

For this old Yankee dessert, mix together 2 cups milk, ¼ cup minute tapioca, ½ teaspoon salt and ⅔ cup maple syrup. Cook over hot water for 15 minutes, stirring frequently. Separate 1 egg. Beat yolk well. Stir a few spoonfuls of hot milk mixture into beaten yolk, and continue stirring to prevent curdling. Add rest of hot mixture and stir for 3 minutes over hot water. Cool; add ½ cup chopped nutmeats. Beat egg white and fold into mixture. Pour into bowl and cool; refrigerate until served, plain or with whipped cream. Serves 6.

Olde Grist Mill, Kennebunkport

On Mill Lane, off State Highway 9, this unique eating place is housed in an old tidewater grist mill which has been owned and operated by the same family since 1749. Lunch and dinner served daily in the delightful dining room overlooking the Kennebunk River. Closed on Monday; reservations advised. Open June 20 through the Sunday before Labor Day. Painting by Alois Fabry.

Golden Corn Cake

3/4 cup corn meal
1 cup flour
1/3 cup sugar
3 teaspoons baking powder
1/2 teaspoon salt
1 cup milk
1 egg, well beaten
2 tablespoons melted shortening

Mix and sift dry ingredients; add milk, egg and shortening. Bake in 8-inch-square greased pan in 350° oven for 20 minutes.

Baked Indian Pudding

Pour 2 cups scalding milk on 1/3 cup corn meal; cook in double boiler for 20 minutes. Add 1/2 cup molasses, 1/2 cup sugar, 1/4 cup butter, 1 teaspoon salt and 1 teaspoon ginger or cinnamon. Pour hot mixture into buttered pudding dish, then pour in 2 cups cold milk. Do not stir. Set in a pan of hot water and bake 3 hours in 250° oven. Top warm pudding with ice cream or with sweetened whipped cream. Makes 6 generous portions.

Boone's Restaurant, Portland

Located on picturesque Custom House Wharf, Boone's is justly famous for its fine seafood, especially for Maine lobsters fresh from its own pound across the street. The interior of Maine knotty pine paneling and the turquoise-and-white checkered tablecloths make for perfect "Down East" dining. Lunch and dinner from 11:30 A.M. to 9:00 P.M.; closed Sunday. Reservations necessary for large groups. Painting by Laurence Sisson.

Angel Fish Loaf with Lobster Sauce

1½ pounds raw halibut, ground
1½ cups soft bread crumbs
1 cup hot milk
1 teaspoon baking powder
1 teaspoon celery salt
1 teaspoon salt
1 teaspoon pimento, minced
2 egg whites, beaten stiff

Make a paste of the bread crumbs and hot milk. Add the halibut, baking powder, celery salt, salt and pimento. Mix well. Fold in beaten egg whites. Turn into a small bread tin (3½ x 7½ x 3 inches), which has been greased and lined with waxed paper. Place the tin in a shallow pan of water and bake at 350° until firm and lightly browned, about 45 minutes. Serve in slices with the following sauce:

Sauce

Sauté meat from 1¼ pound lobster (about 8 ounces lobster meat) in 2 teaspoons butter in a heavy skillet. Add 1½ cups medium white sauce, well seasoned, and ¼ teaspoon paprika. Heat thoroughly. Makes 4 servings.

O Sole Mio, Skowhegan

Red candles in Chianti bottles and famous actors from nearby Lakewood Summer Theatre are among the charms of Doris Veneziano's family-style Italian restaurant, on the highway many travelers take to Quebec City. It is located on U.S. 201 two miles north of Skowhegan. The menu features braciola, baked lasagna, and other dishes which originated in Italy and are made from recipes that have been in the family for many years. Open 10:00 A.M. to 1:00 A.M. the year round, closed on Sundays from mid-November to mid-May, and on Christmas Day. Reservations for dinner advisable during summer season. Painting by James Carpenter.

Braciola (Beef Rolls)

2 pounds top round steak, $\frac{1}{2}$ inch thick
1 clove garlic, finely chopped
1 tablespoon Parmesan cheese, grated
1 green pepper, chopped
2 slices salt pork, cut fine
$\frac{1}{2}$ teaspoon salt
$\frac{1}{4}$ teaspoon black pepper
$\frac{1}{4}$ cup olive oil
1 small onion, chopped
$2\frac{1}{2}$ cups tomatoes, sieved
$\frac{1}{2}$ teaspoon salt
$\frac{1}{4}$ teaspoon pepper
1 bay leaf

Lay out steak and wipe with clean damp cloth. Cover steak with mixture of garlic, cheese, green pepper, salt pork, salt and pepper. Roll up steak to enclose mixture and tie securely. Cut into 4- or 5-inch portions. Heat olive oil in a large, heavy skillet and cook onion for a few minutes. Add steak rolls and slowly brown on all sides. Combine tomatoes, salt, pepper and bay leaf and slowly add to browned steak. Cover skillet and simmer about $1\frac{1}{2}$ hours or until steak is tender. Remove string and bay leaf. Slice and serve. Serves 6.

Jimmy's Harborside Restaurant, Boston

The cry of sea gulls, tangy salt-water breezes and the excitement of historic Boston Fish Pier make a perfect setting for this famous seafood eating place. Open for lunch and dinner daily except Sunday, it is at 242-266 Northern Avenue. James and Charles Doulos are the owners. Painting by Alois Fabry, Jr.

Baked Stuffed Fillet of Sole

1   pound lobster meat
2   pounds grey sole fillets (7-8 ounces per slice)
3   slices white bread, trimmed and chopped fine
3   teaspoons cracker crumbs
1/2 pound butter
2   ounces sherry
1   teaspoon grated Parmesan cheese
3   tablespoons flour
12 ounces warm milk
8   ounces warm cream
paprika and salt, to taste

Stuffing

Mix chopped bread with cracker crumbs, 1/8 pound melted butter, 1 ounce of sherry, 1 teaspoon grated cheese, adding a pinch of salt and then half of the lobster-meat.

Newburg Sauce

Sauté 3 tablespoons of flour in 1/8 pound melted butter, adding 8 ounces warm milk and 8 ounces warm cream. Simmer until it thickens, then add salt and pinch of paprika. Sauté remainder of lobster meat with very little butter, add 1 ounce of sherry and mix with sauce.

Spread each fillet with stuffing and roll up. Place in pan with a little butter in bottom, add 4 ounces of milk and salt slightly. Bake in 350-degree oven for 25 minutes. When ready to serve, pour the Newburg sauce over the fillets. Serves 4.

The Mad Hatter, Nantucket

On Easton and Beach streets on Nantucket Island, this restaurant in a weathered shingle house features an atmosphere that is as informal as its hardwood floors and its sturdy wooden tables and chairs. Lunch and dinner served daily. Reservations necessary. Richard Parker and Earle Smith are the owners and chefs. Painting by C. Robert Perrin.

Coquilles Saint Jacques

Poach 1 pound fresh scallops in 1 cup dry white wine for 5 minutes. At same time sauté 3 shallots in ¼ cup butter until transparent. Add 1 pound cooked lobster and 1 pound cooked and cleaned shrimp to shallots. In another pan sauté ½ pound fresh mushrooms in ¼ cup butter. To this add 1 tablespoon each of chopped chives and parsley. When mushrooms are cooked add 1 tablespoon brandy and flambé mixture. Add scallops to lobster and shrimp mixture. Season with 1 teaspoon ginger, a few grains cayenne pepper, 1 tablespoon salt and 1 tablespoon dry mustard. Scald 1 quart light cream and thicken with 4 tablespoons moistened cornstarch and cook until thick. Slowly add 3 lightly beaten eggs to cream, then add mushrooms and cook for 5 minutes over low fire, stirring constantly. Fold this sauce into fish mixture. Place in large casserole or individual ramekins. Cover with grated Parmesan cheese and brown under broiler. Serves 6–8.

Méditerranée, North Truro

This delightful Cape Cod restaurant is in a 150-year-old house built by a sea captain. Mr. and Mrs. George Beiers are the hosts at this country-type eating place which prides itself on an attractive décor, friendly service and excellent food, with emphasis on Continental dishes. Take U.S. 6 to North Truro. Turn off at Highland Road exit, continue west on Highland Road. This restaurant is 300 yards from U.S. 6 on Pond Road, which is a continuation of Highland Road. Open for dinner on Saturdays only in early spring and fall. Dinner served every day 6:00 P.M. to 10:00 P.M. from July 1 through September 4. Reservations advisable. Painting by Arthur Barbour.

Spinach Omelet

1 1/2 tablespoons olive oil
2 tablespoons chicken stock
1 packet frozen whole spinach
pepper to taste
1/2 teaspoon salt
1 clove garlic chopped fine
4 tablespoons freshly grated Sardo or Parmesan cheese
10 eggs
2 tablespoons water
2 tablespoons butter

Place oil and stock with spinach in saucepan. Break up spinach. When spinach has softened add pepper, salt and garlic. Simmer gently for twenty minutes. Add cheese, stir and simmer 5 more minutes. Beat eggs and water lightly in a bowl, add pinch of salt and pepper; melt butter in a 10-inch skillet and when butter is hot pour in beaten eggs. Keep moving wet mixture in from edge with a spatula until all the egg mixture is almost cooked. Spread spinach across half of omelet and fold other half over it. Turn omelet out onto a warm dish and serve immediately. Serves 4.

The Wayside Inn, South Sudbury

The poet Longfellow described this charming inn, two miles west of South Sudbury, Massachusetts, on U.S. 20, in this way: "As ancient is this hostelry as any in the land may be, Built in the old colonial Day..." In 1923 it was purchased by Henry Ford and furnished with rare antiques, an adjacent wing also being added, which contains the Ford dining room. Open for breakfast, lunch, tea, and dinner daily, except Christmas Day. Overnight accommodations available; reservations recommended. Painting by Glenn MacNutt.

Wayside Inn Chicken Pie

Cut up a 4-5-pound stewing hen and place in a kettle. Cover with boiling water. Add to kettle: a couple of sprigs of parsley; 3-4 stalks celery with leaves on; 1 whole carrot; 1 slice onion; 1 tablespoon salt and a dash of pepper. Bring to a boil for 2 minutes, then lower heat and simmer gently for 2-3 hours. Cool, then remove meat from bones in large pieces. Place chicken pieces in 1 large casserole or 6 individual casseroles. Add 2 cups pearl onions and 1/2 cup of peas. Strain broth and to each 4 cups of broth add 1/2 cup of flour combined with 1 cup of milk to form a paste. Cook until thickened. Season with salt and pepper, to taste. Add to casserole. Cover with pie crust or a rich biscuit dough and make large slits in crust. Bake at 450° till crust browns and serve at once. Serves 6-8.

The Oaks Inn, Springfield

This charmingly restored homestead, located on Route 20 (upper State Street) in Springfield, Massachusetts, is a haven for gourmets. It features an open-air porch for summer dining and an outdoor merry-go-round bar. Smorgasbord served every Sunday from noon to 8 P.M. except holidays. Managed by Thomas L. Sophinos, the restaurant serves breakfast, lunch and dinner seven days a week the year round. Painting by W. A. Hanley.

Lobster Stuffed with Lobster

Take two small, live lobsters. Boil one for 15 minutes, then remove the meat from the tail and claws. Mix thoroughly $1/2$ cup coarse cracker meal, $1/4$ cup dry bread crumbs, 1 tablespoon each of dried celery leaves and Hungarian paprika, add $1/4$ cup unsalted butter and the cooked lobster meat. Split the second lobster for broiling and crack the claws. Place mixture of boiled lobster and crumbs on top of split lobster, leaving tail exposed. Broil at lowest position of broiler and continually baste with unsalted butter until stuffing turns golden brown. Remove from broiler and bake at 450° for 10 minutes. Serve with drawn butter and lemon. Serves 1.

Red Lion, Stockbridge

First open to the traveling public as a coach stop in 1773, this charming New England hostelry is still a popular stop for travelers who want an excellent meal or an enjoyable vacation. On Main Street (U.S. Highway 7), it serves breakfast, lunch and dinner daily. Overnight accommodations in the main building or adjacent motor lodge; recreational facilities. Open May 28 to October 25. Eugene Webb is the manager. Painting by Paul Decker.

Breast of Chicken Perigourdine

Melt a small amount of butter in a large skillet, then brown 3 or more chicken breasts, halved, on both sides, adding more butter as needed. Remove, add more butter to skillet and sauté 8 large mushrooms which have been sliced. Remove mushrooms. Into butter, stir 1/3 cup all-purpose flour, 1/4 teaspoon salt, 1/4 cup dried mushrooms (soaked in water for 1 hour), 1 cup chicken broth, and 2 tablespoons light cream. Cook, stirring over medium heat until thickened and smooth. Place chicken in sauce and simmer gently for about 20 minutes, or until chicken is tender. Meanwhile make about 2 cups of Hollandaise sauce and refrigerate it. When chicken is tender add 3 tablespoons sherry and sautéed fresh mushrooms. Spread cold Hollandaise over chicken and place under broiler for about 1 minute or until just golden. Serve at once. Serves 6.

Black Lantern Restaurant, near Keene

A fine 18th-century colonial house and its spreading wing contain a series of delightful dining rooms. In season, open daily except Monday for lunch and dinner; from November 1 through March, luncheon served only on Sunday. Reservations appreciated. Located five miles south of Keene on Route 12. Painting by William Hanley.

Bread

Scald 2 cups milk and pour into a large bowl; then add 2 tablespoons sugar, 2 teaspoons salt, and 2 tablespoons shortening. Stir until shortening is melted. Cool until lukewarm. Crumble 1 yeast cake or packet of dry yeast into ¼ cup lukewarm water and stir until softened. Add 6 cups flour, 1 cup at a time; mix thoroughly after each addition. Add more flour if necessary until it forms into a ball and does not stick to the bowl. Turn the dough onto a lightly floured board and knead gently for about 3 minutes. Brush top of dough with oil or butter and set in warm place, 80-85°, until dough doubles in bulk or impression remains when lightly pressed with fingers. Then press dough down and cut dough in half. Form 2 loaves of bread, pulling cut edges under until each loaf is smooth and rounded on top. Place in 2 greased loaf pans, 9 x 5 x 3 inches. Brush again with oil or butter; set to rise in warm place until double in bulk. Bake in preheated 400° oven for about 40 minutes. When done, loaves shrink away from the pan and have a hollow sound when tapped. Remove from pans and place on wire rack to cool. Makes two 1-pound loaves.

Wayfarer Motor Inn, Manchester

Located just an hour's drive from Boston, this vacation complex is easily recognizable to motorists by its Early American Shaker design. Breakfast, lunch and dinner served daily. Overnight accommodations and recreation facilities are available. The Inn is situated at the junction of Routes 3 and 101 and the Everett Turnpike. Leave the Turnpike at the Bedford exit. The Dunfey family own and manage the Inn. Painting by C. Robert Perrin.

**Roast Duckling
with Bing Cherry Sauce**
2   4-pound ducklings
stuffing for ducklings
1   No. 2¹/₂ can pitted Bing
    cherries
¹/₂ cup red port wine
1   tablespoon cornstarch

Stuff both ducklings with your favorite stuffing recipe. Roast in 325° oven on racks for 2¹/₂-3 hours, or until tender. Drain cherries, reserve juice, add wine to liquid. Bring liquid to boil and thicken with cornstarch which has been mixed with cold water. Return cherries to sauce and bring to a boil. Split roasted ducklings in halves, lengthwise. Top with hot cherry sauce. Serves 4.

Green Ridge Turkey Farm Restaurant, Nashua

Famed as "New England's Favorite Restaurant," this fine eating place is on U.S. 3, south of Nashua. Specializes in New Hampshire turkey, along with oysters, roast beef, steak and lobster. Open for lunch and dinner, seven days a week from 11:30 A.M. to 10:00 P.M. Painting by Adele Bichan.

Turkey Oriental

1/2 cup slivered, blanched almonds
3 tablespoons butter or margarine
1 teaspoon salt
1 small clove garlic, minced or mashed
2 cups cooked turkey, cut in pieces
1 can (5 ounces) water chestnuts
1 small can (3 ounces) sliced mushrooms
1/2 cup each, pineapple chunks, chopped green pepper, diced fresh tomato
1 cup diced celery
6 green onions, thinly sliced
1 tablespoon each, sugar and cornstarch
4 tablespoons soy sauce

3 cups hot rice or crisp Chinese noodles

In a large heavy frying pan, brown the almonds in 1 tablespoon of the butter; remove nuts with a slotted spoon and set aside. Add remaining 2 tablespoons butter to the pan with salt, garlic, and turkey; cook, stirring, until browned. Drain and save liquid from water chestnuts and mushrooms. Add 1/3 cup of this liquid to the pan with sliced water chestnuts and mushrooms; cover and cook 5 minutes. Add pineapple, peppers, tomato, celery, green onion, and half of almonds; cook and stir 5 minutes. Blend sugar, cornstarch, soy, and 1/4 cup more reserved liquid; stir into hot mixture; cook until thickened. Garnish with rest of almonds. Serve on rice or noodles. Serves 6.

Historic Smithville Inn, near Absecon

Inspired by the historic past of the Inn — it was a stage coach stop in 1787 — owners Mr. and Mrs. Fred Noyes, Jr., restored it and then began a reconstruction of 18th century stores, buildings and craft shops. Noontime buffet served week days 11:30 A.M. to 2:30 P.M.; regional country dinner 4:00 P.M. to 10:00 P.M.; Sunday dinner noon to 9:00 P.M. The Inn is six miles north of Absecon on U.S. Highway 9. Painting by Howard Connolly.

Deviled Crab
1   pound back fin crabmeat
3   tablespoons butter
2   tablespoons onion, minced
2   tablespoons flour
³/₄ cup hot milk
¹/₂ teaspoon salt
1   teaspoon dry mustard
¹/₈ teaspoon red pepper
1   teaspoon Worcestershire sauce
1   tablespoon parsley, chopped
1   egg beaten into 1 cup milk
1   cup breadcrumbs
deep fat for frying

Pick over crabmeat carefully, removing all bits of spine or shell. Sauté onions in butter until tender. Add flour and stir until mixture is smooth. Add hot milk gradually and cool until thickened. Add seasonings only after mixture is removed from fire. Stir crabmeat into mixture. Shape into patties. Dip into milk-and-egg mixture and then into breadcrumbs. Fry in 350° deep fat until golden brown. Makes about six 3-ounce cakes.

Lucien's Old Tavern, Berlin

Once a stagecoach stop, this historic old hostelry at 81 W. White Horse Pike (U.S. 30) in Berlin, New Jersey, is just 15 miles east of the Benjamin Franklin Bridge in Philadelphia. Lunch and dinner served weekdays; open Sunday for dinner at 3:00 P.M. Lucien P. Fleche is the owner and manager. Painting by Albert Gold.

Lobster Thermidor "Rothermel"
Boil four 2-pound lobsters and cool in shells. Remove lobster meat from shells and cut into bite-size pieces. Sauté 1/2 pound sliced mushrooms in 4 tablespoons of butter. Over slow heat, slowly blend in 4 tablespoons of flour, salt and pepper to taste, a dash of Tabasco and 1 teaspoon Worcestershire sauce. Combine lobster and 1 pint light cream into smooth sauce, simmer, then stir in 1/4 pound *freshly grated* Parmesan cheese. Flatten the lobster shells, fill with creamed mixture, which should be the consistency of thick cream sauce (if too thick, add milk sparingly). Sprinkle tops with breadcrumbs, butter dots and 1/4 pound Cheddar cheese, crumbled. Place under broiler for 3 minutes or until lightly brown, and serve. Serves 4.

Rod's 1890's Ranch House, Convent Station

A popular part of this restaurant is the Parlour Car Lounge, which is located in a completely restored 19th century Pullman car. All of the original brass fittings were left intact, and the cut velvet draperies and gold rope portières are faithful replicas of those in vogue when the car was built. The dining rooms are in a conventional building and serve lunch and dinner every day. Guests are seated in order of arrival. Situated on New Jersey Highway 24, Convent Station, which is near Morristown. Painting by Crawford Livingston.

Grenadines of Beef Tenderloin Flambé Rissolda

4 medallions of prime beef tenderloin (2 ounces each)
1 shallot, chopped fine
2 ounces butter
1 mushroom, sliced thin
1¹/₂ ounces Burgundy wine
3 ounces brown sauce or brown gravy
1¹/₂ ounces cognac

Dust medallions with flour. Melt butter in sauté pan and brown meat. Remove and keep warm. Add shallot and mushroom to sauce in pan and cook lightly. Add Burgundy and reduce contents of pan. Add brown sauce and barely bring to a boil. Place medallions in preheated flambé pan and sauce in separate serving dish. Pour brandy into flambé pan and ignite. Baste medallions until flame dies. Remove meat to dinner plate. Add sauce to flambé pan and bring to high heat. Spoon sauce over half of each medallion. Makes 1 generous portion. It is served here with buttered broccoli flowerettes and soufflé potatoes.

Bahr's Restaurant, Highlands

Converted from a boathouse into a popular shoreside eating place in 1890, this restaurant is still a favorite for fresh seafood dinners, steaks and chicken. The dining room overlooks the Shrewsbury River, and there are complete facilities for boaters to dock. Automobiles turn off New Jersey Route 36 at Highlands Bridge to 2 Bay Avenue in Highlands. Lunch and dinner served daily. Closed on Monday. Painting by Howard Connolly.

Bahr's Special
1/2 pound cooked king crab meat
1/2 pound boiled scallops
1/2 pound cooked shrimp, coarsely chopped
1/2 pound lump crabmeat
2 tablespoons minced Spanish or Bermuda onion
1 cup melted butter
2/3 cup flour
2 cups milk
1/2 teaspoon white pepper
1 tablespoon salt
1 cup dry sauterne

1/2 cup whipped heavy cream

First prepare **Supreme Sauce:**
Sauté onions lightly in butter; add flour and mix well, then add milk, pepper, salt, and wine. Cook over slow heat until thickened. Set aside 1/2 cup of sauce and add to it whipped cream, to be used as topping. Mix all seafood with balance of sauce and spoon into large clam shells. Cover with topping and bake for 12 minutes at 350°, or until brown. Serves 6–8.

Bottle Hill Restaurant, Madison

The pretty town of Madison, now within commuting range of Newark and New York, was once an important stagecoach stop known as Bottle Hill. The original posthouse, built in 1812, has been carefully preserved since a visit in 1825 by the Marquis de Lafayette, and now houses an excellent restaurant. Located on Main Street (State Highway 24) in Madison, it is open every day for lunch and dinner. Reservations necessary. Painting by Helen Fleming.

Frog Legs Rissolé Provençale

1 cup flour
1/2 cup milk
1/2 teaspoon salt
1/4 teaspoon pepper
3 pounds frog legs
1 cup vegetable oil
2 cups stewed tomatoes
dash of lemon juice
3 cloves garlic, chopped very fine
1/4 pound butter
few sprigs parsley, chopped

Mix flour, milk, salt and pepper in a bowl. Dip frog legs in this mixture. Sauté in frying pan with the vegetable oil until golden brown — about 10 minutes. Place stewed tomatoes on a hot platter and arrange frog legs over them. Add dash of lemon juice. Keep in warm oven. Brown garlic in butter and pour over dish. Top with chopped parsley. Serves 6.

Aurora Inn, Aurora-on-Cayuga

A delightful country inn established in 1833, the Aurora is located on the eastern shore of Lake Cayuga, twelve miles south of U.S. Highway 20 on New York State Highway 90. Owned and operated by Wells College, it serves meals daily from 8:00 A.M. to 10:00 A.M., noon to 2:00 P.M. and 6:00 to 8:00 P.M. Overnight accommodations and vacation facilities are available. Closed December 20 to January 5. Painting by Charles Harper.

Brownies

2 eggs
1 cup sugar
²/₃ cup cooking oil
1 cup flour
¹/₂ teaspoon salt
¹/₂ teaspoon baking powder
2 squares chocolate, melted
¹/₂ cup nuts, chopped
1 teaspoon vanilla

Beat eggs, add sugar, then oil. Sift in flour mixed with salt and baking powder. Add melted chocolate, vanilla and nuts. Bake in greased 8-inch square pan for 20 minutes in 350° oven.

Coconut Cream Pie Filling

Combine in a double boiler: 3 cups scalding milk; 1 cup sugar; 5 level tablespoons cornstarch; ¹/₂ teaspoon salt; 3 egg yolks; 1¹/₂ teaspoons vanilla; ¹/₂ cup macaroon-type coconut. Cook until mixture thickens, stirring constantly. Cool, then pour into 9-inch baked pie shell.

Meringue

Beat 3 room-temperature egg whites until very stiff, slowly adding ¹/₂ cup sugar. Cover pie. Bake 10 minutes at 400°.

Peacock Inn, Mayville

For more than a century the Inn has stood on its wooded promontory at the head of Lake Chautauqua among green timbered hills. Dinner served daily 5:30 P.M. to 10:00 P.M.; Sundays and holidays 12:30 P.M. to 7:30 P.M. Owner Anthony de Mambro suggests reservations. His inn is located on Route 17J (20 North Erie Street) six miles from New York Thruway exit 60. Painting by Peter Gilleran.

Breast of Chicken à la Peacock

8- to 10-ounce boneless breast of chicken
1 ounce sweet butter (pressed into elongated egg shape)
egg wash (beat together: one egg, $\frac{1}{3}$ cup milk, pinch of salt)
breadcrumbs
vegetable oil
1 slice French toast
1 slice baked ham, $\frac{1}{8}$ inch thick

Place breast of chicken on cutting board and slice off about $\frac{1}{4}$ of top portion. Flatten both pieces with cleaver. Place butter on larger bottom portion and cover with smaller piece. Seal together with fingers. Flour entire piece well, dip into egg wash and roll in breadcrumbs. Preheat frying pan with thin layer of vegetable oil. Place chicken breast in pan and sauté on both sides about one minute on open flame. Remove from open flame and place in 400° oven, bake for 10 minutes on both sides. Place French toast on serving dish, topped with the slice of ham, and then add chicken. Serve with brown mushroom gravy and sprig of parsley. Serves 1.

Brasserie, New York City

The keys to the doors were thrown away the day this popular restaurant in midtown Manhattan opened, and since that time the Brasserie has served hearty meals and good wine 24 hours a day. Otto Meier, a 28-year-old Swiss-born chef, created a distinctive and varied Alsatian menu. The elegant modern interior of the restaurant blends with the functional lines of the Seagram Building at 100 East 53rd Street, which houses it. Painting by Cecile Johnson.

Gâteau Côtes De Chevreuil
3 ounces almond paste
4 egg yolks
vanilla extract, to taste
3 ounces bitter chocolate, melted
3 egg whites
pinch of salt
4 tablespoons sugar
4 tablespoons sifted flour

Soften almond paste, add yolks slowly and beat. Add vanilla extract and melted chocolate. In separate bowl beat egg white with salt and sugar. Fold ⅓ of egg white mixture into the almond paste. Add flour to this and remaining egg white. Pour into greased loaf mold approximately 9″ x 3″ x 2″. Bake in 400° oven 20 to 25 minutes. Cool, cut cake lengthwise, and fill with Chocolate Butter Cream Filling.

Filling
Blend together: ¼ pound butter; 3 tablespoons sugar; pinch of salt; and ½-ounce bitter chocolate. When mixture is smooth spread over bottom layer of split cake and replace top. Then pour 3 ounces melted bitter chocolate over entire cake. Serves 12.

Café Chauveron, New York City

This small, superb restaurant at 139 East 53rd Street serves classic French dishes prepared under the direction of one of the owners, Roger Chauveron. Open weekdays for lunch and dinner; reservations necessary. Closed Sundays and the month of July. Painting by John Kuller.

Salmon Parisienne

4-5 pounds salmon, sliced thick
1/2 cup vinegar
1 large onion, sliced
1 large carrot, sliced
2 sprigs parsley
2 stalks celery
2 bay leaves
1/2 teaspoon thyme
1 tablespoon salt
8 peppercorns
1 lemon, sliced

Place salmon in a large saucepan, add remaining ingredients, except lemon slices, with water to cover. Simmer until boiling. Remove from fire and let cool. When cool remove salmon from the pan, take out the bones and remove skin. Place salmon slices on a large platter, then place lemon slices and parsley around the platter for decoration. Serve cold with any kind of vegetable salad. Mayonnaise, tartar sauce or Russian dressing may be served with salmon. Serves 6.

Charlie Brown's Ale and Chop House, New York City

A warm and friendly dining room done in the style of a turn-of-the-century English pub. Emphasis is on the chophouse atmosphere, with roast beef and Yorkshire pudding at lunch and dinner. Open noon to 1:00 A.M. every day. Closed on Sunday. It is in the main concourse of the Pan American Building, 200 Park Avenue. Painting by John Kuller.

Beef and Kidney Pie

- 1/2 pound veal kidneys, cut into small pieces
- 2 pounds chuck of beef, cut into cubes
- 2 ounces shortening
- 3 ounces flour
- 2 ounces tomato purée
- 2 chopped onions
- 1 cup red wine
- 1 cup mushrooms, cut in quarters
- 2 ounces butter

Put kidneys in pot, cover with water, let them come to a boil, rinse them well in cold water. Brown the beef cubes in 2 ounces of shortening, add the kidneys. When well browned, sprinkle the flour over the meat, mix well, add tomato purée, chopped onions, red wine, and water or beef broth to cover. Cover pot and let stew simmer about 2-2 1/2 hours. Sauté the mushrooms in butter for 5 minutes, add them to the stew, season with salt and pepper. Put the stew in individual pot-pie dishes and cover with rolled-out puff pastry. Beat 1 egg yolk and brush over the crust; bake at 375° for 20 minutes. Serves 6.

Scotch Eggs

Divide 1 pound of lean ground pork into 6 portions. Shell 6 hardboiled eggs. Enclose each egg in a coating of ground pork. Beat 2 raw eggs lightly, coat each egg in beaten raw eggs and roll in breadcrumbs. Fry in 350° deep fat until pork is cooked and each egg is golden brown. Place on bed of parsley; serve with tomato relish. Serves 6.

Jager House, New York City

One of Manhattan's famous neighborhood restaurants, Jager House features German food with a Viennese accent—the schnitzels, sauerbraten, sausages and pastries, prepared under the direction of Chef Noel Vaz. Open every day from noon until midnight, Saturday to 1:00 A.M. The address is 1253 Lexington Avenue, near E. 85th Street. Painting by Marvin Friedman.

Jager House Beef Goulash
- 6 pounds shin or stewing beef, cut in 1-inch cubes
- 6 pounds onions, chopped fine (or better, grated)
- $1/2$ cup vegetable shortening
- 1 pint unsalted beef stock or water
- 3 cloves garlic, crushed
- pinch of freshly ground pepper
- $1/2$ cup sweet Hungarian paprika
- $1/3$ cup tomato purée
- salt to taste
- boiled potatoes or noodles

Brown meat very carefully in 350° oven, keeping watch so that meat does not dry out. Sauté onions in vegetable shortening until golden. Place browned meat in heavy pot with beef stock, garlic, onions, pepper, paprika, tomato purée and salt, to taste. Cook covered on top of stove over low fire for $2^{1}/_{2}$ to 3 hours, or until tender. Add stock or water during the cooking if more liquid is needed. Serve over hot noodles or boiled potatoes. Serves 10–12.

La Fonda Del Sol (Inn of the Sun), New York City

This unique and beautiful restaurant, located at 123 West 50th Street, in the Time-Life Building, offers world-famous Latin-American cuisine, featuring steak and roasts from the Argentine as well as food from Mexico, Peru, Brazil, and Chile. Hundreds of folk-art objects and symbols of the sun are displayed in the dining rooms. Open every day for luncheon and dinner; reservations necessary. Painting by Alois Fabry.

Barbecued Leg of Lamb
8-pound leg of lamb

Have butcher bone leg of lamb, place in combined marinade ingredients for about 4 hours. Grill over open charcoal pit, till charred on both sides to retain juices. Cook to desired degree of doneness. Serve with favorite bar-becue sauce, rice and Sangría Wine Punch.

Marinade
Combine 10 ounces lemon juice, 6 ounces olive oil, 2 tablespoons salt, 1 tablespoon cracked pepper, 1 clove garlic, 8 shallots or green onions, 1 tablespoon coriander, 1 tablespoon monosodium glutamate and a pinch of Italian or Cayenne pepper.

Sangría Wine Punch
Make syrup by adding 1 cup sugar to 2 cups water. Heat, stirring until sugar is dissolved; bring to boiling point. While still hot, add 1 each of thinly sliced orange, lemon and lime. Marinate for at least 4 hours before using. Place about 12 ice cubes in a pitcher with 6 marinated fruit slices and $1/2$ cup of syrup. Then add 1 bottle Chilean wine, red or white, and about 8 ounces of seltzer water. At serving time place 2 slices of fruit in each glass and fill from pitcher.

Laurent Restaurant, New York City

One of New York City's truly fine French restaurants, this establishment is also noted for its elegant dining rooms and polished service. It is located in the Lombardy Hotel at 111 East 56th Street. Lunch and dinner served daily; dinner only on Sunday from 5:00 P.M. Reservations necessary. Closed on Sunday during July; in August closed both Saturday and Sunday. Painting by Harvey Kidder.

Gazpacho Andaluz

Liquefy 1 garlic clove and 1 medium onion in a blender. Add: 5 very ripe tomatoes; 2 sprigs parsley; 2 tablespoons vinegar; 3 tablespoons olive oil; $1/4$ teaspoon paprika; 1 cup beef stock or consommé. Run blender at high speed for 2-3 minutes. Season to taste with salt and pepper. Place in soup tureen and refrigerate. Then serve in chilled bowls with separately chopped cucumber, tomato, green pepper, green onions and croutons, as condiments. Serves 6.

Chocolate Pots de Crème

Scald 2 cups cream with 1-inch piece of vanilla bean, 4 ounces melted sweet chocolate and $1/4$ cup sugar; cool slightly. Beat 6 egg yolks until light and lemon-colored, then add cream, stirring constantly. Strain mixture through fine sieve and pour into 6 small earthenware pots or custard cups. Set in pan of water, cover and bake in 250° oven for 15 minutes or until a knife inserted in the center comes out clean. Serve chilled. Serves 6.

Lobster Box Restaurant, New York City (City Island)

The oldest landmark on City Island, this fine seafood restaurant is housed in a century-old mansion, and the two dining rooms overlook Long Island Sound. Specialties are shore dinners, steamed clams, lobster served 21 ways — and steaks and chops. All food is cooked to order. Open 5:00 P.M. to 11:00 P.M.; Sunday 1:00 P.M. to 10:00 P.M. Closed on Monday. Reservations advisable on weekends. The address is 34 City Island Avenue. Painting by Harvey Kidder.

Lobster Newburg

1½ cups cooked lobster meat, diced (about 3 small lobsters)
2 tablespoons butter
½ tablespoon flour
½ cup light cream
3 tablespoons of cream sherry
2 egg yolks, lightly beaten
½ teaspoon salt
pinch of cayenne
4 patty shells, or crisp toast

Sauté lobster meat in melted butter over low heat for 5 minutes. Sprinkle in flour, add cream slowly, stirring constantly until sauce boils. Add sherry and egg yolk, and cook for about 1 minute. *Do not overcook,* because sauce will curdle. Season with cayenne and salt. Serve in patty shells or over toast. Serves 4.

Mama Leone's, New York City

Since 1906, this restaurant in the heart of the theater district has been famous for warm hospitality, gay music and fine Italian food. Open every weekday from 4:30 P.M. to 1:00 A.M. On Sunday and holidays, dinner is served 2:00 P.M. to 10:00 P.M. Reservations necessary. The address is 239 West 48th Street. Painting by Al Tiegren.

Saltimbocca alla Romana

Have 1¼ pounds veal cutlet sliced very thin and cut into 3-inch squares. Slice 1 standard-size mozzarella cheese similarly. Cut 4 ounces prosciutto (Italian ham) into 3-inch squares. Cut 7 small truffles into small pieces. On one square of veal place 1 piece of mozzarella, 1 piece of prosciutto, 1 piece of truffle, a pinch of sage, another piece of mozzarella and cover with another piece of veal. Fasten with toothpick. Repeat process until all squares of veal have been used. Melt 3 tablespoons butter in 5 tablespoons olive oil in deep saucepan. Brown veal well on both sides; put aside. In same frying pan add: ¼ cup celery, chopped; 1 large clove garlic, chopped; 1 large onion, chopped; 1 medium carrot, chopped. Season to taste with salt and pepper. Cover; simmer about 10 minutes or until carrots are soft. Add 1 pound peeled tomatoes and cook until moisture evaporates. Gradually add one cup dry sherry into which 2 tablespoons tomato paste have been blended. Stir occasionally to prevent burning. Cover; simmer over low flame for 30 minutes. Drain sauce and pour over Saltimbocca. Serves 4–6.

Paradise Oriental Restaurant, New York City

This Greek restaurant, one of the best in New York City, is across the street from the Port Authority Bus Terminal at 311 West 41st Street. Among its specialties are Cheese and Spinach Pie and a variety of lamb dishes. Open daily, 11:00 A.M. to 11:00 P.M., for lunch and dinner. Painting by Marvin Friedman.

Spinach and Cheese Pie

1 large bunch fresh dill (about 6 tablespoons chopped)
1 large bunch Italian parsley
6 scallions
2 pounds fresh spinach
1 cup olive oil
6 eggs
1 pound feta cheese, crumbled
1 pound phyllo pastry (obtainable in Greek specialty shops)

Marinate in olive oil chopped dill, parsley and scallions (include scallion tops). Cook spinach very briefly, pour cold water over to stop the cooking and drain well. Add thoroughly drained spinach to olive oil. Beat eggs, add crumbled cheese. Add egg and cheese mixture to spinach, oil and herbs. Line a large (11 by 14 inches) baking pan with half the phyllo pastry, brushing it well with melted butter or oil. Place spinach filling on pastry and cover with remaining pastry, again brushing well with melted butter. Seal edges of pastry. Bake in 300° oven for 45 minutes or until well browned. Cut into squares. Makes 16 generous servings.

San Marino Restaurant, New York City

Many gourmets feel that this fine restaurant serves some of the best northern Italian food available in Manhattan. It is located at 236 East 53rd Street and is open weekdays for lunch and dinner. Reservations necessary. Closed on Sunday. Painting by Howard Connolly.

Broiled Shrimp à la Tony
12 large unshelled shrimp
1 clove garlic, cut
1 teaspoon salt
1/2 teaspoon pepper
1 cup olive oil or salad oil
2 tablespoons lemon juice
Slit unshelled shrimp down backs, cutting 3/4 way through. Remove sand veins. Marinate shrimps for 2 hours in mixture of remaining ingredients. Place shrimp on a broiling pan and pour marinade over shrimp. Broil 7-8 minutes. Turn once. Serves 4 as an appetizer.

Monblason Inn, Pine Plains

Charles Virion is both chef and owner of this country inn which specializes in French haute cuisine. Advance reservations necessary for meals and rooms. Breakfast, lunch and dinner served daily. Closed first two weeks in February. It is on Willowvale Road, 1¹/₂ miles east of Pine Plains in Dutchess County. Painting by Harvey Kidder.

Chocolate Soufflé
2   squares unsweetened chocolate
¹/₃ cup superfine sugar
3   teaspoons instant coffee
¹/₃ cup hot water
2   tablespoons flour
4   tablespoons sweet butter
1   cup scalded milk
1   tablespoon vanilla extract
4   egg yolks
7   egg whites
2   tablespoons superfine sugar

Melt chocolate in double boiler, add sugar and stir, then mix in coffee mixed with hot water. Make a smooth white sauce with butter, flour and milk and combine with chocolate mixture.

Cool until just warm and then stir in the egg yolks, mix well, and add the vanilla. Beat the egg whites until stiff, but not dry, add 2 tablespoons superfine sugar, beat one more minute and fold in the chocolate sauce. Pour in a well-greased 2¹/₂-quart soufflé dish. Bake 5 minutes in preheated 375° oven, then reduce heat to 350° and bake 20 minutes longer. Serve topped with Crème Chantilly, below. Serves 6.

Crème Chantilly
¹/₂ pint whipping cream
1   teaspoon very fine sugar
1   teaspoon pure vanilla extract

Beat until stiff.

The Witherill — A Treadway Inn, Plattsburgh

Opened in 1868, this fine small hotel in downtown Plattsburgh has been owned and operated by the Howell family for more than 80 years. Although most of the original building has been replaced, some of the old furnishings have been retained and such features as the black walnut and butternut trim in the Green Room were saved. Breakfast, lunch, and dinner are served daily in the two dining rooms from 7:00 A.M. to 10:00 P.M. Overnight accommodations. Painting by Hugh Laidman.

Home Corned Beef with Vegetables

2¹/₂ pounds beef brisket
2 tablespoons salt
2 tablespoons pepper
1 tablespoon ginger
1 clove garlic
1 teaspoon saltpeter
4 peeled potatoes
6 carrots, cleaned
¹/₂ head of cabbage

Rub brisket of beef on all sides with mixture of salt, pepper, and ginger. Place beef in 4-quart stone crock and add whole garlic clove and saltpeter. Pour cold water in crock to cover. Let this preparation stand 10 full days in crock in cool place or refrigerator. Take beef from crock and simmer in brine for about 2 hours or until tender. Add potatoes, cabbage and carrots and cook for 45 minutes until tender. The entire brisket may be cooked at one time and leftovers used for cold corned beef. Serves 4.

Patricia Murphy's Candlelight Restaurant, Yonkers

On a hill surrounded by award-winning gardens, this popular restaurant is at 1703 Central Park Avenue. It is two miles north of New York Thruway exits 5 northbound and 6E southbound, and about 20 miles north of New York City. Lunch and dinner served daily; closed only on Christmas day. (There are two other Patricia Murphy restaurants in downtown Manhattan.) Painting by Dom Lupo.

Rum Chocolate Cream Pie

4 cups milk, divided
2 tablespoons butter
1 cup sugar
2 squares unsweetened chocolate, melted
6 tablespoons cornstarch
4 egg yolks, slightly beaten
2 tablespoons rum
$^1/_2$ teaspoon salt
1 10-inch baked pie shell
1 cup whipping cream

Combine $^3/_4$ cup milk, butter, and sugar. Stir over low heat until mixture comes to a boil. Add melted chocolate; mix well. Blend cornstarch to thin paste with a little of the cold milk, then stir in remaining cold milk, and add to chocolate mixture slowly while stirring. Cook and stir until well thickened, then cook for another 10 minutes without stirring. Add hot mixture to egg yolks, and mix well. Return to saucepan, add salt, cook and stir for 1 minute. Remove from heat, add rum, and spoon into baked pie shell. Chill until firm. Whip cream, and swirl onto pie. Top with shaved bittersweet chocolate.

Erculiani's Restaurant, Gallitzin

Although the menu here is predominantly Italian, excellent Continental dishes discovered by the Erculiani family while traveling in Europe are also featured. Dinner is served from 4 P.M. to 9 P.M. every weekday; noon to 7 P.M. on Sundays and holidays. Closed from December 1 to March 1. The address is 600 Tunnelhill Street in Gallitzin, on the western slope of the Allegheny Mountains. Turn off the Pennsylvania Turnpike at the Bedford exit (No. 11), take U.S. Highway 220 to Duncansville intersection, then go five miles west on U.S. Highway 22. Painting by Ben Eisenstat.

Casata à la Erculiani

2 8-inch-square layers of sponge cake (each about 1¼ inches thick)
4 teaspoons rum
2 cups thick dark chocolate pudding
4 teaspoons Anisette
2 cups thick vanilla pudding
chopped cherries and nuts

Place one cake layer in bottom of pan. Sprinkle with rum. Spread cake with chocolate pudding; cover with second layer of cake. Sprinkle this layer with Anisette and then cover with vanilla pudding. Garnish with chopped cherries and nuts. Chill for at least 2 hours before serving. Cut into squares. Serves 12–16.

George Winkler's Steak House, Providence

A popular and friendly restaurant in downtown Providence which is famous for its fine steaks, chops and lobsters — as well as its Continental dishes. George Winkler is the owner of this establishment, which is open every weekday for lunch and dinner; reservations necessary. Closed on Sunday and the first two weeks in July. The address is 34 Middle Street. Painting by Al Albrektson.

Breast of Chicken Cordon Bleu
whole breast of a 4-pound chicken
2 thin slices cooked ham
2 slices Swiss cheese
salt, pepper, and paprika
Worcestershire sauce
1 egg, well beaten
1 cup fine breadcrumbs
1/2 cup flour
1/2 cup salad oil
1 cup tomato sauce or basic
   white cream sauce
Split breast of chicken in half, bone completely, and flatten each half. On half of each chicken breast place slice of ham and Swiss cheese, sprinkle with paprika and season with salt, pepper and a few drops of Worcestershire sauce. Fold chicken pieces over, flour each side well and dip into beaten eggs and roll in fine bread crumbs. Preheat shortening in a heavy skillet over medium heat and sauté chicken until well browned on each side. Serve topped with hot tomato sauce or white sauce, which should be fairly thin. Makes 2 portions.

The Mansion House, Providence

This restaurant is a recreation of a famous 18th-century hotel in the area and is a part of the Sheraton Biltmore Hotel located in downtown Providence on U.S. Highways 1, 6 and 44. The main dishes of the restaurant are based on early American recipes and feature local favorites — johnnycakes, fish chowders, quahaug pies and littleneck cocktails. Lunch and dinner served daily; hot foods served to 11:00 P.M.; open until 1:00 A.M. Closed on Sunday. Overnight accommodations in the hotel. Painting by Al Albrektson.

Curry Sauce
1 onion, chopped
1 celery stalk, chopped
1 bay leaf
1 garlic clove, chopped
pinch of thyme
2 ounces butter
2 ounces flour
2-3 teaspoons hot curry powder
4 cups chicken stock
1 ripe tomato, crushed
1 apple, chopped
1/2 banana, chopped
1/3 cup chutney, chopped

Salt to taste
Add onion, celery, bay leaf, garlic and thyme to butter in a heavy skillet. Sauté till onion is golden. Work in the flour, which has been mixed with the curry powder, set over low heat until smooth; gradually add stock, stirring constantly. Cook until thickened. Add remaining ingredients except chutney and simmer for 20 minutes. Strain, season with salt to taste, and add chutney. Serve hot with seafood and rice. Garnish with grated coconut.

Bank Café Restaurant, Warwick

Gene and Frank LaCasio own and manage this eating place located at 40 Post Road (U.S. Highway 1A) in Warwick. It is open every weekday for lunch, dinner and late supper. Reservations necessary. Closed on Sunday. Painting by Al Albrektson.

Boneless Stuffed Chicken
2 broilers, boned and halved
¼ cup white rice
¼ cup brown rice
2 tablespoons butter
½ cup chopped or sliced
mushrooms
2 tablespoons poultry seasoning
salt and pepper to taste
oil
paprika
½ cup dry white wine
Boil combined rice 15-18 minutes in salted water. In skillet melt butter and sauté mushrooms until tender. Combine rice, mushrooms, poultry seasoning, salt and pepper to make a dressing. Place ¼ of dressing between breast and thigh of each chicken half. Fold leg flesh over and press firmly together to keep dressing intact. Place breast side up on greased baking pan. Brush each chicken piece with oil. Sprinkle with paprika. Baste occasionally with wine. Roast at 375° for 55-60 minutes or until done. Serves 4.

Four Chimneys, Bennington

Surrounded by three acres of rolling landscaped lawns and garden, this fine eating place is on State Highway 9 (one mile east of U.S. Highway 7) in Bennington, Vermont. Lunch and dinner served every day during the season. Open April 30 to December 1. Painting by Marion Huse.

Calves' Sweetbreads Financière
2 pounds calves' sweetbreads
1 cup onions, diced
1 cup carrots, diced
1 cup celery, diced
scant teaspoon thyme
3-4 ounces butter, melted
$^{1}/_{2}$ cup dry white wine
2 cups brown stock sauce

Garnish
1 cup cooked baby onions; 1 cup sautéed mushrooms; 1 cup thick smoked bacon pieces fried crisply; 1 cup green olives, pitted and salt to taste.
Wash sweetbreads and boil for approximately 10 minutes, remove from fire and run under cold water until cool. Remove all muscles and membranes from them. Spread onions, carrots and celery evenly over bottom of a baking pan and sprinkle with thyme. Place sweetbreads over vegetables close together and place in 450° oven for 5 minutes. Glaze sweetbreads with butter, then add wine and continue cooking in oven for 15 minutes. Add brown stock sauce and return to oven and bake 15 more minutes. When done, remove pan from oven, place sweetbreads in serving dish and keep warm. Strain sauce from original baking pan and season with salt. Simmer for 10 minutes. Add garnish to sauce and simmer for a few minutes, then pour over sweetbreads and serve immediately. Serves 4.

Lamplighter Steak House, Brattleboro

Owner Nicholas Gladke says that his restaurant is the original steak house in the state, but seafood is also featured on the menu. Take No. 3 exit on Interstate 91 in Brattleboro and go about a quarter of a mile north on U.S. 5 (Putney Road) to the restaurant. Open every day for breakfast and dinner; on Monday nights from 5:00 P.M. to 10:00 P.M. there is a special buffet. Overnight accommodations, with pool and large play area; reservations appreciated.

Shrimp Chablis
1 pound large shrimp, cooked and shelled
5 tablespoons butter
4 tablespoons onion, chopped
pinch garlic salt
salt and pepper, to taste
1 teaspoon cornstarch
4 tablespoons Chablis
6 tablespoons beef consommé
2 tablespoons parsley, chopped
2 cups very dry cooked rice

Heat butter in a large skillet. Add onion and sauté for a few seconds. Add shrimp and sauté until heated through. Add garlic salt, salt and pepper and stir in the cornstarch. Add wine and heated consommé and simmer gently until slightly thickened. Add parsley just before serving over rice. Serves 4.

Coffee Rum Parfait
Pour 1 cup very hot coffee over 10 ounces small marshmallows, mix until almost melted. Mix in 1 ounce dark rum, then fold in 1 cup heavy cream, whipped, and pour into 5 parfait glasses. Let stand 30 minutes, then refrigerate or freeze for several hours. Top with whipped cream. Serves 5.

Toll Gate Lodge, Manchester Depot

Diners on the covered or enclosed dining terrace view a delightful cascading brook and a woodland scene of great natural beauty. The owners, Barbara and Mario Berry, offer a continental cuisine of excellent quality. The lodge, which is housed in the oldest and last toll house in Vermont, is open for dinner only; reservations advisable. Open May 27 until weekend following Columbus Day. It is four miles east of U.S. 7 and Manchester Center on State Highways 11 and 30, in Manchester Depot, Vermont. Painting by Alice Schafer.

Sauce Smitane
1 small onion, sliced
1 tablespoon butter
1 cup dry white wine
2 tablespoons Béchamel sauce
1 tablespoon meat extract
1 cup heavy cream
juice of 1 lemon

Sauté onion lightly in butter. Add wine and cook until wine evaporates, about 10 minutes. Add remaining ingredients, stir constantly on strong fire until volume is reduced to approximately 1 pint. Pour through fine sieve. Excellent over breast of guinea hen, capon or over game.

Town & Country Motor Lodge, Stowe

Another of the growing number of combined four-season resorts and convention motor lodges, this one is in Stowe on Mountain Road, just a mile west of Route 108 toward Mount Mansfield. The Rib Room is the inn's largest dining room and features a waterfall and brook as a part of the décor. Breakfast and dinner served daily. Overnight accommodations and recreational facilities. Stu Ireland is the manager. Painting by Richard Wagner.

Town & Country Cheesecake

2 pounds cream cheese
9 ounces granulated sugar
3 egg yolks
vanilla and salt to taste
grated rind and juice of one orange
3 whole eggs
4 ounces sour cream
6 ounces Cheshire cheese, finely grated
1 cup graham cracker crumbs

Mix cream cheese into a smooth paste; add sugar and egg yolks, vanilla, salt, orange rind and juice. Add whole eggs, sour cream, and Cheshire (or Cheddar) cheese. Line a deep cheesecake tin, 9-inch diameter, with graham cracker crumbs. Pour the cheesecake mix into the pan and bake at 350° for 75 to 80 minutes. Let stand in oven. Top with pineapple sauce when serving.

Pineapple Sauce

Cut a fresh pineapple in cubes, sprinkle some sugar on it (keep sauce fairly tart), and let the pineapple soak for an hour; then add some lemon juice and keep in refrigerator until serving time.

The Trapp Family Lodge, Stowe

Baroness Maria Augusta von Trapp, whose life story was the basis for the hit musical *The Sound of Music,* supervises the dining room of this picturesque inn, located three miles outside of Stowe, Vermont, off Route 108. Tourists can ski on nearby Mount Mansfield, then enjoy Austrian delicacies amid the beautiful surroundings. Painting by Stuart Eldredge.

Zwetschkenknoedel

2 pounds potatoes
$1/2$ pound flour
2 tablespoons butter
$1/4$ tablespoon salt
12 small blue plums

Boil potatoes and mash them. Then while they are still warm, work them together with the flour, butter and salt. With fingers dusted with flour, flatten dough out to thickness of about $1/4$ inch and cut into 5-inch squares. Place a whole plum in center of each and fold dough over to form a sealed ball. Place these plum dumplings in boiling salt water. They will rise to the top when finished. Remove from water, roll in additional melted butter, then in sweet breadcrumbs (made by putting $3/4$ cup breadcrumbs in $1/4$ cup butter mixed with 1 teaspoon sugar and 1 teaspoon cinnamon) and serve hot. Serves 4–6.

Woodstock Inn, Woodstock

An inn since 1793, this historic hostelry is located on the village green on U.S. 4, in the center of the village of Woodstock. Open for breakfast, lunch and dinner daily. Overnight accommodations and recreation facilities. Reservations advisable first two weeks of October and during Christmas holidays. Painting by Arthur J. Barbour.

Fried Breast of Fowl

Select six 4- to 6-ounce breasts of chicken or capon and simmer slowly in seasoned water (1 sliced onion, 4 stalks celery) until done. Then roll in flour, dip in beaten egg and roll in cracker meal. Fry in deep fat at 375° until golden brown. Serve in a bed of rice topped with Supreme Sauce.

Supreme Sauce

Take 4 cups of stock in which fowl was simmered and bring to a brisk boil. Dissolve 3 tablespoons cornstarch in 1/2 cup additional stock (cold) and stir into boiling stock. Stir until it thickens. Remove from heat. Add salt and pepper to taste. Blend 2 egg yolks into 1 cup of cream, stir into sauce. Serve hot.

Vermont Pumpkin Pie

Combine: 1 3/4 cups pumpkin, 2 eggs, 3/4 cup sugar, 1/2 teaspoon salt, 1 teaspoon cinnamon, 1/2 teaspoon ginger, 1/4 teaspoon cloves and mix thoroughly. Then stir in 1 2/3 cups evaporated milk, mix and let stand 15 minutes. Pour into flaky unbaked 9-inch pie shell. Bake at 400° for 30 minutes or until center is firm.

Walper Hotel, Kitchener

Joseph Zuber, Jr., owner and manager of this establishment, represents the third generation of his family to operate the hotel and its excellent dining rooms. At the intersection of Provincial Highways 7 and 8 in downtown Kitchener, the address is 1 King Street West. Breakfast, lunch and dinner served daily; reservations preferred. Overnight accommodations. Painting by Ralph Avery.

Beef Stew in Beer

3 pounds short ribs or shoulder of beef
¹/₂ pound onions, diced in large pieces
4 ounces lard
¹/₃ ounce salt
pinch of paprika
1¹/₄ pounds peeled tomatoes, pressed to remove seeds
1 cup water
1¹/₄ pounds potatoes, sliced
6 ounces beer

Cut beef into half-inch slices. Combine meat and onions and sauté in lard over moderate fire until onions are golden. Season with salt and paprika. Add tomatoes and ¹/₃ cup water. Cover and cook in oven for 1¹/₂ hours. Add remaining water and potatoes. Continue to cook in oven, basting often. Do not stop basting until the liquid is entirely reddened. When finished, add beer. Serves 6.

The Westbury Hotel, Toronto

In the heart of Toronto's business district, midway between Bloor and downtown shopping centers, this fine hotel has a motor entrance as well as in-hotel parking. Inquire about special family plan rates. The dining rooms here are open daily 7:30 A.M. to 3:00 P.M., and from 6:00 P.M. to 11:00 P.M. Reservations advisable for overnight accommodations and dining room. Owned by the Knott Hotel Corporation, the hotel is at 475 Yonge Street. Painting by Robert Ihrig.

Short Ribs of Beef Pot-au-Feu
5 pounds short ribs of beef
1 pound carrots
1 pound turnips
3 leeks
1/2 head of cabbage
beef stock
pepper and salt, to taste
4-5 boiled potatoes, cut in half if large
chopped parsley mixed with fine rock salt or coarse salt

Pour enough stock over short ribs to cover completely, and cook covered over low heat for 3 hours. The last hour add carrots, turnips, leeks and cabbage (cut in large pieces). Serve piping hot with boiled potatoes in a casserole. In a separate dish serve parsley and salt. Serves 4–5.

Quiche Lorraine
6 slices cooked ham
6 slices Swiss cheese
4 whole eggs
1 cup rich cream
salt and pepper to taste
nutmeg
9-inch pie crust, 1 1/2 inches deep, baked

Arrange slices of ham and cheese alternately in the pre-cooked pastry shell. Mix eggs and cream, and season with salt and pepper. Pour mixture into pie shell and bake in 375° oven for about 45 minutes or until custard is set. Serve hot. Serves 8.

La Saulaie, Boucherville

One of the most beautiful in the Montreal area, this restaurant is on the south shore of the St. Lawrence River with an excellent view of the Seaway for both indoor and outdoor diners. Easily accessible from downtown Montreal by four bridges or the Trans-Canada tunnel, it is at 1161 Marie Victorin (Highway 3), Boucherville. Open every day, lunch from 11:30 A.M. to 3:30 P.M.; dinner 5:30 P.M. to 1:00 A.M. Reservations necessary. Claude La Barre is the manager. Painting by John Petts.

Tournedos St. Laurent

2 tablespoons oil
6 tablespoons butter
4 beef filet mignons, 8 ounces apiece
2 tablespoons shallots, cut fine
2 tablespoons parsley, chopped
salt and pepper, to taste
20 ounces canned white asparagus

Heat oil and 2 tablespoons butter in a frying pan. Sear meat on both sides over a very hot fire, then reduce heat for 4-5 minutes additional cooking, for rare. Drain cooking grease, then put remaining butter in pan and heat until golden brown. Remove frying pan from fire, add shallots, parsley, salt and pepper; shake pan to mix. Cut each filet slantwise in 4 pieces and place on hot plate in overlapping slices. Pour hot butter sauce over meat and garnish with hot asparagus spears. Makes 4 generous portions.

Café Henry Burger, Hull

Madame Burger presides over this cosmopolitan restaurant which is only a short distance from the Parliament Buildings in Ottawa, Canada. Visitors may enjoy the excellent French cuisine of Chef Werner Ledermann from noon to 10:00 P.M. during the week and from 1:00 P.M. to 8:30 P.M. on Sunday. The restaurant is at 69 Laurier Street, in Hull. Painting by John Walsh.

Mignon Cutlets of Veal Parisienne
Cut 6 veal cutlets of leg of veal about $3/8$-inch thick and about 3 inches in diameter. Salt and pepper the cutlets, turn them in flour, and sauté them in butter until done and lightly brown on both sides, about 5 minutes. Arrange on platter and cover with sauce below.

Sauce
To the same pan in which you cooked your cutlets add 1 cup of sliced fresh mushrooms and 1 shallot, chopped. Brown very lightly. Sprinkle 1 teaspoon flour over it, mix well. Pour in $1/2$ cup Madeira wine and 1 cup of demi-glaze or beef stock. Cook for a few minutes and then add $1/2$ cup whipping cream. Let simmer for 2 minutes. Pour hot sauce over cutlets, sprinkle with chopped parsley. Serve with rice, noodles or boiled potatoes. Serves 3–4.

Au Pierrot Gourmet, Montreal

The cozy atmosphere of a little French inn pervades this excellent eating place with its scenes of France on the wall, red-checked table-cloths and candlelight. In the heart of Old Montreal at 421 Notre Dame Street, East, it is open for lunch and dinner every weekday from 11:00 A.M. to 2:00 A.M. Closed on Sunday. Owner-manager Jean-Louis Larré prefers reservations in order to give customers the best service. This chicken recipe originates from the birthplace of the owner — the "Pays Basque" country of France. Painting by John Walsh.

Poulet Basquaise

3-4-pound roasting chicken,
  cut in 6 pieces
2 onions, in small pieces
4 green peppers, in small pieces
6 tomatoes
6 large mushrooms
2 garlic buds, crushed
8 ounces dry white wine
salt and pepper to taste
cognac
parsley

Brown chicken pieces, remove from pan. Brown onions, then add green peppers. When cooked add tomatoes, peeled and seeded, and cook for 5 minutes. Add mushrooms and 2 crushed garlic buds. Cook until all juice is evaporated; add white wine and seasonings. Place chicken in a pan, cover with sauce and heat to boiling point. Cover and place in 350° oven for 45 minutes. Serve on long dish sprinkled with cognac, add parsley when serving. Makes 4 portions.

Café Martin, Montreal

One of the "in" places for the residents of Montreal, this excellent restaurant is housed in what was once a fine old mansion at 2175 Mountain Street, just around the corner from the Ritz in downtown Montreal. Open every day from noon to midnight. Painting by John Petts.

Chicken 21

Place a few sprigs of parsley and a bay leaf inside a 5-6 pound stewing chicken. Place bird in deep kettle and cover with boiling water. In addition to salt you may add onions, celery, carrots, bay leaves, thyme and parsley. Simmer chicken until tender. Remove chicken to hot platter. Strain broth through a fine sieve.

Make a Béchamel sauce by melting 3 tablespoons butter in a saucepan over moderate heat without letting it brown. Add 3 tablespoons flour and stir until it is well blended. Whip in 1 egg yolk, then slowly add chicken broth, stirring constantly. Continue cooking until thickened.

Remove meat (white meat preferably) from bones and cut into large pieces. Add meat to the sauce and let simmer for a while. Place in ovenproof casserole with cooked wild rice — chicken at one end and rice at the other end of the casserole. Sprinkle with Parmesan cheese and bake in 450° oven for 5 minutes. Makes 6 generous portions.

Chez Bardet, Montreal

One of the finest restaurants in a city noted for excellent food, this establishment is run by André Bardet, a master chef, who came to Canada from France nine years ago. At 591 Henri Bourassa Boulevard East, it is across the street from the last stop on the new Metro. Open from noon to midnight weekdays; until 1:00 A.M. Saturdays, and closed on Sunday. Reservations advisable. Painting by Henry J. Simpkins.

Chicken au Gratin

Bone 4 chicken breasts, roast in 300° oven — slightly undercook. Arrange chicken in ovenproof dish. On top of each portion of chicken place a small slice of ham and 2 or 3 Endives Meunières (see below). Cover this with juice from chicken, then sprinkle chicken with 1 cup grated Gruyère cheese. Cook in 400° oven until golden and serve very hot. Makes 4 large portions.

Endives Meunières

Wash 12 small Belgian endives well and place in buttered casserole. Add juice of 2 lemons, let them boil over a flame, then cover with foil and a lid. Bake in 300° oven for 1 hour, then drain them and cook slowly in a pan of melted butter until brown.

Chez Desjardins, Montreal

In the heart of Montreal at 1175 McKay street, this fine seafood restaurant has been popular with gourmets since it opened in 1892. Open daily for lunch and dinner until 2:00 A.M. Closed on Christmas Day. Reservations necessary. Painting by John Walsh.

Dover Sole au Vermouth

6 Dover sole, 14 ounces per fish
6 ounces butter, flaked
6 dried shallots, finely chopped
salt and pepper, to taste
1½ cups French vermouth
1½ cups Béchamel Sauce
6 ounces whipping cream

In a shallow baking dish place sole, butter, dried shallots, salt, pepper and vermouth. Simmer uncovered in 375° oven for 10-15 minutes. When cooked, take fish from liquid and remove all bones. Place fish on warm service platter. Mix remaining liquid in pan with Béchamel Sauce and whipping cream; pour mixture over sole. Before serving glaze swiftly under broiler. Serve with tossed salad and parsley boiled potatoes. Makes 6 generous portions. Recipes for Béchamel vary; following is the one used at Chez Desjardins:

Béchamel Sauce

Make a roux of 3 tablespoons melted butter and 3 tablespoons flour. While beating vigorously add 1½ cups scalded milk, all at once. When it comes to a boil, lower heat and simmer 5 minutes. Season to taste with salt, pepper and pinch of nutmeg.

La Crêpe Bretonne, Montreal

The owners, Mr. and Mrs. Tavan, both from France, have been in Canada for 15 years. The idea for this restaurant, which is actually the middle section of three tiers of restaurants under the same management, came from Josette Tavan who decided to reproduce an old Breton Inn in midtown Montreal. One of the specialties is pancakes, but also famous are the special onion soup and Cheese Fondue. Located at 2080 Mountain Street, it is open from 11:00 A.M. to 2:00 A.M. every day. Painting by John Walsh.

"Louis" Cheese Fondue

Melt 1 teaspoon of butter in a casserole. Pour in 10 ounces of white wine. Let it warm. Crumble 1 pound of Swiss cheese (or use $^1/_2$ Swiss and $^1/_2$ Parmesan) and add a handful at a time. Mix until creamy. Add salt and pepper, and a few drops of kirsch. Have your French bread previously cut in large cubes. Serve fondue on a heater. Everyone will dip bread in the cheese. (In case one drops the bread, the penalty is a bottle of wine!) Serves 4–6.

Auberge de la Chaumière, Ste-Adèle-en-Haut

This small but extremely elegant French restaurant is housed in an unpretentious log-built house along the main street of Ste-Adèle-en-Haut, a ski town about 50 miles north of Montreal. Norman-born Mr. and Mrs. Jean-Charles Liorel are the owners. Dinner only; reservations advised. Closed 15 days after Easter and November 10 to December 6. Painting by John Walsh.

Gala Chez le Cardinal des Mers
Prepare court bouillon with dry white wine, well seasoned. Boil 1 hour. Put in 4 live lobsters, weighing 2 pounds apiece. Boil 20-25 minutes. Let cool in bouillon. Take 1 cup of bouillon from lobsters and cook 1 dozen large shrimp in it for 8 minutes. Let cool. Boil together 8 ounces fine dry white wine, 8 ounces water, salt, pepper, chopped onion, bay leaf, 1 tablespoon butter, and the juice of a small lemon. Cook 1 1/2 pounds Dover sole filets in this, gently, without boiling. Remove and keep warm. Do the same in turn with 12 oysters, 12 mussels, 16 scallops and 4 slices of Alaska crabmeat. Keep this liquid and strain. Remove pincers from cooled lobsters. Crack shell of these and remove flesh with- out breaking. With strong scissors, cut the lobsters up the back, making a large, long oval opening. Remove the flesh in 1 piece and cut in slices. Clean out the shell. Make a Béchamel sauce with the bouillon in which the sole was cooked, combined with 2 cups of thick cream. Beat until smooth. Arrange shells on a large platter. Put some sauce in the bottom of each shell. Arrange filet of sole in each. Add a little sauce. Place in each lobster shell 3 oysters, 3 mussels, 3 shrimps, 4 scallops and a slice of crabmeat. Cover well with sauce. Then arrange lobster meat on top. Cover with remaining sauce. Top with grated Emmenthal cheese and pieces of butter. Cook in 350° oven to heat lobster and lightly brown cheese. Serves 4.

Alabama

Delaware

District of Columbia

Florida

Georgia

Kentucky

Maryland

North Carolina

South Carolina

Tennessee

Virginia

Virgin Islands

You hear the ring of history in this lovely land where bountiful feasts are a tradition. The visitor can enjoy modern versions of old plantation favorites, but he can as easily order exotic foreign dishes such as Tak Bok Kum (Korean-style chicken) at one of the increasing numbers of cosmopolitan eating places. Southern fried chicken with hot biscuits is still a regional favorite, but look also for Baked Carolina Country Ham, Stuffed Flounder, Eggbread, Rum Cream Pie. The list goes on and on.

Painting by Richard Wagner

SOUTHEAST

Gulas Restaurant, near Mobile

For over 20 years the three Gulas brothers have operated this fine restaurant on U.S. Highway 90 about four miles west of downtown Mobile. Open every day from 11:00 A.M. to midnight; Sunday hours from 11:00 A.M. to 9:00 P.M. Fish specialties are favorites with the patrons, but Chinese, Greek and German chefs impart a cosmopolitan air to the menu. Painting by Mal Eno.

Stuffed Crab

1½ ounces butter
4 tablespoons onion, minced
1½ teaspoons parsley, minced
1½ sprigs fresh thyme, minced, or ¼ teaspoon dried
½ clove garlic, minced
2 pounds lump crabmeat
1 cup medium-coarse breadcrumbs
2 hard-boiled eggs, chopped
½ cup milk
5 ounces light cream
1½ teaspoons salt
¼ teaspoon black pepper
⅛ teaspoon Cayenne pepper
4 drops Tabasco

Melt 1 ounce butter in a large heavy skillet, then add minced onion, parsley, bay leaf, thyme and garlic and cook for about 5 minutes. Then mix in crabmeat, breadcrumbs and chopped eggs. Remove from fire and cool. In another pan combine milk, cream and ½ ounce of butter and heat, *but do not boil.* Add salt, peppers, and Tabasco. Then add this mixture to cooled crab mixture, folding in gently. When mixtures are thoroughly combined, place in 12 crab shells, 6 ramekins or individual shell servers. Sprinkle with a few bread crumbs and a few dots of butter. Bake in 350° oven until top browns and serve piping hot. Serves 6. This crab recipe is also used as a stuffing for lobster and flounder.

Villula Tea Garden, Seale

An old-fashioned flower garden surrounds this country tearoom, owned by Mrs. Robert Joerg, which is south of Seale on U.S. Highway 431. Most of the vegetables served in the dining room are raised on the grounds. Open for breakfast, lunch and dinner every day. Overnight accommodations. A shop on the grounds sells home-canned foods such as pear and peach preserves, cabbage and artichoke pickles, and dozens of varieties of jams and jellies. Painting by Logan Bleckley III.

Pickled Shrimp
Add boiling water to 2½ pounds of shrimp to cover. Then add 6 celery tops, 3½ teaspoons salt and ¼ cup mixed pickling spices. Cook shrimp 10 to 12 minutes. Drain shrimp and cool with cold water. Peel under running water. Alternate shrimp and sliced onions (1 pint) in shallow dish. Add 7 or 8 bay leaves. Cover with sauce.

Sauce
Combine 1¼ cups salad oil, ¾ cup white vinegar, 2 teaspoons salt, ½ teaspoon celery seed and 2½ tablespoons capers with juice, and a dash of Tabasco. Mix well and pour over shrimp dish. Cover and store in refrigerator for at least 24 hours. Will keep for a week. Served as an appetizer, will yield 20 portions.

The Glasgow Arms, Glasgow

This fine restaurant, located on U.S. 40 ten miles south of the Delaware Memorial Bridge in Glasgow, Delaware, 2 miles on 896 from Newark exit (Interstate Rte. 95), uses the coat of arms of Glasgow, Scotland, on its crest by permission of the Lord Provost of Scotland. Many antiques are displayed in every room, including fine collections of firearms and pewterware. Lunch and dinner are served daily; closed on Sunday. Reservations are necessary for Saturday. Painting by Jerome Kaplan.

Crabmeat Imperial
1/2 medium green pepper, minced
4   stalks parsley, minced
1   pint mayonnaise
pinch white pepper
2   pounds backfin crabmeat

Sauté green pepper and parsley until soft, then fold into mayonnaise and white pepper. Gently stir in crabmeat, breaking as little as possible. Arrange in 5 casseroles and broil until nicely browned. Then place on hot plate until slightly brown around edge or hot entirely through center. Serves 5.

Broiled Tenderloin en Brochette
Cut 4 2-inch-square pieces of beef tenderloin. Blanch 3 large mushroom caps. Season meat and mushrooms to taste with salt and pepper. Alternate meat on skewer with mushroom caps, broil to desired taste, basting with butter and sherry. Place on platter of fried rice. Serves 1.

The Genghis Khan Restaurant, Washington, D.C.

Chefs formerly with embassies turn out gourmet dishes of Japan, Korea, China, India, Thailand and Indonesia at this elegantly appointed dining room at 1805 Connecticut Avenue, N.W. Spectacular house specialties are volcano soup, Tak Bok Kum, and "Mauna Loa Chicken"—a meal cooked at your table. "Looks like Vesuvius," says owner Bill Lee. Lunch and dinner served daily. Reservations necessary. Painting by Alice Acheson.

Tak Bok Kum (Korean Style Chicken)

2 broiler chickens, disjointed
1 cup Japanese soya sauce
1 cup dry Sherry
1 tablespoon garlic powder
1 teaspoon ginger powder
2 teaspoons monosodium glutamate
1 cup green onions, chopped
2 tablespoons sesame oil or crushed sesame seeds

Combine all ingredients and marinate chicken for at least 4 hours. Can be marinated for up to 48 hours. Broil skin side down, then turn. Cook until not quite done. Dip in sauce and return to broiler skin side up. Cook 5-6 inches below broiler until done. Chicken meat should be very moist with a nicely browned skin. Serves 4.

Golden Parrot, Washington, D.C.

Housed in a fine old mansion built in the 1880s, this restaurant, owned by John Goldstein, still reflects the spirit of the original. The address is 1701-20th Street, N.W. Open for lunch and dinner, except Sunday and holidays. Reservations advisable. Painting by John Heinly.

Baked Stuffed Shrimp

Peel 1 pound uncooked shrimp, leaving tail shell on. Split shrimp down the back and spread apart, butterfly fashion. Dip uncooked shrimp into mixture of $^1/_4$ cup milk and 1 egg, then in mixture of $^1/_2$ cup breadcrumbs and $^1/_2$ teaspoon paprika. Combine: 1 pound lump crabmeat, 1 teaspoon Worcestershire sauce, salt and pepper to taste, dash of Tabasco, 2 tablespoons mayonnaise, 1 teaspoon prepared mustard and 2 slices fresh bread, cubed. Sauté 1 minced medium onion and $^1/_2$ green pepper, finely chopped, in 2 tablespoons melted margarine and add to crabmeat mixture. Firmly stuff breaded shrimp with crabmeat mixture. Place shrimp tail side up on a greased shallow baking dish. Baste shrimp with 3 ounces melted margarine. Bake in 400°F. oven until brown. Serve piping hot. Serves 4.

Luigi's Spaghetti House, Boynton Beach

Patrons say it is worth the trip to this attractive spot just to receive the friendly greeting of the hospitable owner, Luigi Mirisola. Of course, they are certain of an excellent meal of fine Italian food also. Located at 2404 South Federal Highway (U.S. Highway 1) between South Boynton and North Delray, Luigi's is open for dinner every day during the season from 4:00 P.M. to 10:30 P.M. Closed on Wednesdays from June through September. Painting by George Shellhase.

Tortoni Ice Cream

1 quart heavy cream
3 eggs
1 ounce almond extract
1 ounce light rum
1 cup sugar, extra fine if possible
6 macaroons, crushed
8-9 maraschino cherries, cut in half
1/2 cup finely chopped walnuts or pecans
16-18 four-ounce paper cuplets

Place mixing bowl and beaters in refrigerator or freezer until cold. Pour heavy cream in bowl and beat at medium speed until it starts to thicken. Add all the other ingredients except cherries and nuts and beat at high speed until batter forms peaks. Spoon into cups to fill. Pour cherry juice over top for color (if desired), sprinkle with chopped nuts and top with cherry half. Place in freezer until firm and serve. Tortoni may be stored for a long period of time in a freezer. When ready to serve, remove from freezer for 10-15 minutes.

San Remo, Daytona Beach

The airy dining room here features a tree growing in the center as well as unusual tropical plants within reach of the tables. Italian and American cuisines are featured. Dinner served every day except Monday. Reservations necessary. At 1290 South Ridgewood (U.S. 1) this restaurant is not far from the beach and the Daytona International Speedway. Painting by Robert Curran.

Veal Scaloppine à la San Remo

Pound 1½ pounds thinly sliced veal cutlets until very thin. Cut veal into pieces about 6 inches square. Sprinkle with salt and pepper and flour lightly. Melt 4 tablespoons butter in large skillet and, when hot, put in veal and brown thoroughly on both sides, over high heat. When well browned add ½ cup Marsala and let meat cook 1 minute. Turn heat down to simmer. Add ½ cup sliced mushrooms; over each piece of veal place a thin slice of prosciutto topped with a piece of thinly sliced mozzarella cheese. Add 4 tablespoons chicken stock and simmer for a minute or so. Place skillet under broiler until the cheese is melted. Serves 6.

Jamaica Inn Restaurant, Key Biscayne

The dining room surrounds a huge, glass-enclosed tropical garden flourishing with equatorial plants. Just 15 minutes from the heart of Miami, it is at 320 Crandon Boulevard on Key Biscayne. The Inn is open for dinner only; however, the English Pub, which is both antique shop and restaurant, is open for breakfast, lunch and dinner year around. Painting by George Shellhase.

Jamaican Ginger Beef

2 onions
3 cloves garlic
1½ teaspoons turmeric
¼ teaspoon dried chili peppers (optional)
5 teaspoons ginger (or 2-inch piece fresh ginger, chopped)
1½ teaspoons salt
1¼ pounds flank steak
3 tablespoons peanut or salad oil
1 No. 2 can tomatoes
10½-ounce can condensed onion soup
4-6 cups hot cooked rice
pickled watermelon, for garnish

In chopping bowl, combine onions, garlic, turmeric, chili peppers, ginger and salt; chop fine. Add flank steak cut diagonally into thin slices or 2-inch by ½-inch strips and toss together. Stand to season in refrigerator from 15 minutes to 3 hours. Heat oil in Dutch oven, add steak and onion mixture and brown lightly. Add tomatoes, then cook uncovered over high heat for 10 minutes. Add soup, cover and simmer 1 hour if steak is sliced; or 1½ to 2 hours if in the thicker strips. To serve, form hot rice in a mound in center of serving platter, spoon a few pieces of the steak over rice then spoon rest of mixture around it. Garnish at both ends with pickle. Serves 4 generously.

The Chatterbox Restaurant, St. Petersburg

At the corner of Central Avenue and First Street in downtown St. Petersburg, this popular restaurant has been in the same location for over 31 years, under the management of the Cowan family. Lunch served daily from 11:30 A.M. to 4:00 P.M.; dinner 5:00 P.M. to 10:00 P.M. Reservations necessary during the winter season; closed on Sundays and Christmas Day. Painting by Robert Chase.

Red Snapper Soup

Smother ¼ cup diced onion, 1 cup diced celery and 1 green pepper, diced, in 2 tablespoons butter combined with 2 pints Fish Stock until mixture comes to a boil. Add 1 pint Tomato and Brown Sauce and bring to a boil again. Add 1 cup diced red snapper and let cook until fish is tender, about 12 minutes. Just before serving add I cup sherry.

Fish Stock

In a kettle put trimmings of the fish —bones, head, fins, etc.—and cover with 3 pints of water. Add: 1 cup dry white wine, 1 medium onion stuck with a few cloves, 6 peppercorns, ½ bay leaf, 1½ teaspoons salt, 2 sprigs parsley, 1 carrot, cut in thin strips, and a pinch of thyme. Simmer for 30 minutes and strain.

Tomato and Brown Sauce

Brown 3 tablespoons flour in ¼ pound of lard. When golden brown add 3 pints of beef or chicken stock and one No. 2 can tomato puree. Cook 2½ hours.

Rollande & Pierre, St. Petersburg

French dishes comparable to any in the country are served at this attractive restaurant at 2221 4th Street, North. Dinner served from 5:00 P.M. to midnight daily, 5:00 P.M. to 11:00 P.M. Sunday; closed Monday. Reservations advisable on Saturday. Rollande and Pierre Loehrer are the owners. Painting by Robert Chase.

Marchand de Vin Sauce
1 pound butter
2 cups Burgundy
$^1/_2$ cup shallots, chopped
$^1/_2$ cup parsley, finely chopped
$^1/_2$ teaspoon black pepper

Let butter stand at room temperature. Heat wine in large saucepan and add shallots, parsley and pepper. Simmer until mixture is reduced to half. Cool and add to the softened butter. Blend well. Mario Loehrer, the manager at this restaurant, suggests letting the finished Marchand de Vin Sauce chill and then forming it into small balls. These can be melted over hot steak, chicken or shrimp at serving time. Serves 6.

The Sand Dollar, St. Petersburg

The location and hours of this popular restaurant make it particularly convenient for motorists. Near Fort DeSoto Park, at 2401 34th Street South (U.S. Highway 19), it is open for lunch and dinner with a special night owl menu offered from 9:30 P.M. to 2:00 A.M. John Dahlberg, Jr., is the manager. Painting by Marion Terry.

Frozen Fruit Salad
orange juice
1/4 cup red maraschino cherries
1/4 cup green maraschino cherries
3/4 cup pecans, broken
3 ounces miniature marshmallows
1/4 cup mayonnaise
1 cup canned fruit cocktail
1/4 cup yellow cling peaches
1/2 cup whipping cream, whipped
2 envelopes unflavored gelatin
Drain juice from fruit cocktail and peaches and add orange juice to make 2 cups of liquid. Soften gelatin in 1/2 cup cold water. Bring fruit juices to boil, add gelatin and stir until dissolved. Combine remaining ingredients and add to gelatin mixture. Pack into container and freeze. Defrost slightly, unmold and arrange slices on lettuce. Can be served with French, piquant or mayonnaise dressing, according to taste, or may be served without dressing if preferred. Serves 12.

Sheraton Inn, St. Petersburg

This luxurious new vacation resort is located on the north end of the Sunshine Skyway Bridge and Causeway (U.S. 19) in St. Petersburg. There are two swimming pools with patios, a children's playground, as well as facilities for boating, fishing and golfing. Breakfast is served in the Kona Room at any hour of the day, and dinner and entertainment are offered nightly in the Tiki and South Seas Rooms. Painting by Marion Terry.

**Cantonese Chicken Livers
à la Outrigger**
2 pounds chicken livers
2 cups soy sauce
2 bay leaves
4 garlic cloves
1 7-ounce can water chestnuts
1 7-ounce can sliced mushrooms
1 tablespoon Burgundy
2 cups chicken stock
1 tablespoon cornstarch
6 toast wedges

Toasted sliced almonds
Marinate chicken livers in soy sauce, bay leaves and garlic for 4 or 5 hours. Sauté chicken livers until browned; add sliced water chestnuts and mushrooms with a dash of Burgundy. To the above combination add chicken stock thickened with cornstarch. Bring to a boil. Simmer until chicken livers are cooked. Serve in casserole on toast wedges. Garnish with toasted sliced almonds. Serves 6.

Whispering Sands Inn, Sarasota

This unusual resort is situated on a 45-acre estate on Siesta Key, with 1,000 feet of beach on the Gulf of Mexico. Overnight accommodations with complete vacation facilities are offered from November 15 to May 15. Dining room open to general public every day from December 15 to April 15. Reservations recommended. It is at 5000 Ocean Boulevard, Sarasota. Painting by Earl Gross.

Chicken Anno

Fold skin around four boned chicken breasts, forming each into a ball. Place chicken in pan, skin side up, brush with butter and season with monosodium glutamate, onion and garlic salt, and paprika. Place in 400° oven and cook for 15 minutes until almost done. Remove from oven and place 2 slices of bacon on each piece of chicken; return to oven until bacon and chicken are done. Make 2 cups thick cream sauce. Season to taste with salt and pepper. Blend in 1 cup grated Cheddar cheese, 3 tablespoons sherry and 1 cup cooked, chopped spinach. Place cooked chicken breasts with bacon in casserole. Pour sauce over chicken. Sprinkle with grated Parmesan cheese and brown under broiler. Serves 8.

Ocean Grill, Vero Beach

On the ocean front at Sexton Plaza, this superior restaurant owned by Jake Replogle has a 20-year reputation for excellent food. It is decorated with art treasures such as the grillwork which is used as a room divider. Open for lunch and dinner every day; lounge open until 1:00 A.M. Closed during September. Reservations necessary. Painting by George Shellhase.

Stuffed Flounder, Ocean Grill
Stuffing
- 1/2 cup small bread cubes
- 2 tablespoons butter
- 2 tablespoons finely chopped onion
- 1/2 cup crabmeat
- salt and pepper, to taste
- 2 flounder fillets, about 1/2 pound each

Sauté bread cubes in butter and then add remaining ingredients, blending well. Place half of stuffing on each flounder fillet. Roll with stuffing inside and secure with toothpicks. Brush lightly with 2 tablespoons melted butter and bake in 400° oven until fish flakes when tested with a fork, about 12-15 minutes.

Sauce
Melt 2 tablespoons butter, blend in 2 tablespoons flour, 1/4 cup fish stock and 3/4 cup light cream, stirring constantly. Cook and stir until thickened and smooth. Season with salt and pepper to taste. Add 1 tablespoon sherry and just before serving add 6-8 whole shrimp. Serve sauce over flounder. Makes 2 large portions.

The Mimosa Restaurant, Baxley

Southern cooking, hospitably served in a family atmosphere, is the specialty of the Mimosa. Regular customers as well as Florida-bound tourists consider this one of the best restaurants in southern Georgia. It is on U.S. 1, just outside Baxley. Okefenokee Swamp Park is within driving distance. Overnight accommodations available. Open daily. Painting by David Reese.

Banana Nut Cake
3/4 cup butter
2 cups sugar
3 large eggs
4 medium bananas
1 teaspoon baking soda
1/2 cup nuts
3 cups flour
2 teaspoons baking powder
1/2 teaspoon salt
1/2 cup buttermilk
1 teaspoon vanilla

Cream butter and sugar well. Add eggs one by one, beating thoroughly after each addition. Add mashed bananas with baking soda. Add nuts. Sift flour with salt and baking powder and fold into batter, alternating with buttermilk. Add vanilla. Beat until smooth. Pour into four 8-inch round cake pans which have been greased. Bake 30 minutes at 350 degrees.

Icing
Mix 2 cups sugar and 1/4 cup white Karo syrup together, add to 1/2 cup boiling water. When the sugar has completely dissolved, remove from heat, cool, pour slowly into stiffly beaten whites of 4 eggs and continue to beat until icing is stiff enough to spread.

The Deck, Brunswick

Overlooking the Marshes of Glynn, on St. Simons Island Causeway at Brunswick, the main dining room is a replica of the deck of a yacht and the décor carries out a marine theme. The Deck is open 11:00 A.M. to 10:00 P.M. daily; summer open 12:00 P.M. to 11:00 P.M.; closed only on Christmas. Specialty is an aromatic dish called Shrimp Mull, concocted at Brunswick, Georgia by Eustas Butts and his cronies. Painting by Harry L. Baker, Jr.

Shrimp Mull

2 No. 2 cans tomatoes
1 No. 2 can tomato soup
1/4 pound butter
1 cup white bacon, diced
1 cup onion, chopped
2 cloves garlic, sliced
1 whole lemon, sliced
1 cup celery, chopped
1 teaspoon celery seed
15 drops Tabasco
1 bottle tomato catsup
2 tablespoons Worcestershire sauce
1/4 teaspoon allspice

1/4 teaspoon curry powder (hot)
5 pounds raw shrimp, peeled
1 cup sherry
1/4 pound butter

Into a heavy kettle put 2 quarts water, canned tomatoes, and tomato soup. Simmer. Melt butter in skillet and brown bacon and onion in it. Add to tomato mixture. Add all remaining ingredients in first column, and boil lightly for 2 hours. Add shrimp and simmer for 1 hour. Add 1 cup sherry and another 1/4 pound butter. Thicken with cracker crumbs. Serve with flaky dry rice. Serves 8–10.

Smith House Dining Room, Dahlonega

When you dine here, you will be seated over a rich vein of gold ore, discovered in 1899 when the foundations of the building were being excavated. It is on State 60, one-half block from the public square in Dahlonega, Georgia, off U.S. 19. Dining room open for all meals daily except Mondays and Christmas Day. Accommodations. Painting by Logan Bleckley III.

Lettuce and Boiled Egg Salad

Combine the following ingredients in a salad bowl: 1/2 head of firm lettuce, broken in pieces; 2 medium onions, sliced in rings; and 6 hard-boiled eggs, sliced. Mix together and pour over salad a dressing made of: 1/2 cup mayonnaise; 1 tablespoon prepared mustard; 2 tablespoons vinegar; 1/2 teaspoon pepper; and 1 teaspoon salt. Toss and serve to 6.

Macaroni and Cheese Casserole

Cook 4 ounces elbow macaroni in boiling salted water until tender. Mix with 3 well-beaten eggs, 1 tablespoon salt and pepper, to taste, 1 cup milk and 1/2 pound grated sharp cheese. (Save some of the cheese to sprinkle on top.) Put in greased casserole and bake at 300° for about 30 minutes, then turn to 400° for a few minutes to brown top slightly. Serves 8.

Town and Country Supper Club, Covington

Dining and dancing under the apple tree in the famous Apple Tree Lounge is one of the features of this popular Covington restaurant which is across the river from Cincinnati, Ohio. There are several attractive dining rooms open for lunch and dinner until 1:00 A.M. every day. Reservations appreciated. The club is at 1622 Dixie Highway (U.S. Highways 25 and 42), just half a mile north of the junction with Interstate 75 — Kyles Lane exit. Glenn Caldwell is the manager. Painting by J. P. Olmes.

Town and Country Special Cake
2 cups cake flour, sifted
2 cups sugar
2 teaspoons soda
2 teaspoons cinnamon
1 teaspoon salt
1 cup vegetable oil
4 eggs
3 cups carrots, shredded
1 teaspoon vanilla

Combine flour, sugar, soda, seasonings and oil. Then beat in eggs, one at a time, carrots and vanilla. Pour into 2 greased 9-inch cake pans. Bake in moderate oven for about 30 minutes. When cool, frost cake with icing prepared as follows:

Icing
Cream together 8 ounces cream cheese and 1/4 pound butter. Add to this 1 box confectioners' 10X sugar, 1 teaspoon vanilla and 1 cup of pecans. Beat until well blended.

Old Stone Inn, Simpsonville

Just a mile from busy Interstate 64 is this 150-year-old former stage-coach stop which still offers excellent Southern home cooking to travelers. It is on U.S. Highway 60 in Simpsonville. Closed from November 1 to April 1. Lunch served 12:30 P.M. to 2:00 P.M., and dinner 5:30 P.M. to 8:00 P.M. The seating capacity is small so it is wise to make reservations. Painting by Jack Kellam.

Stuffed Eggplant
1   large eggplant
$1/2$ teaspoon salt
$1/4$ cup onion, chopped
1   tablespoon butter or margarine
1   tablespoon parsley, chopped
1   $10^1/2$-ounce can condensed cream of mushroom soup
1   teaspoon Worcestershire sauce
1   cup cracker crumbs, very fine
1   tablespoon butter

Slice off one side of eggplant. Remove pulp to within $1/2$ inch of skin. Boil $1/2$ cup of water with $1/2$ teaspoon salt, then add eggplant pulp and cook until tender, about 10 minutes. Drain thoroughly. Cook onions in butter until tender, but not brown. Add eggplant pulp, parsley, soup, Worcestershire and cracker crumbs, except 2 table-spoons. Fill eggplant shell with mixture and place in a 10x6x1$1/2$-inch baking dish. Dot with butter and sprinkle remaining crumbs over the top. Carefully pour 1 cup water into bottom of dish. Bake in moderate (375°) oven for 1 hour or until heated through. Serves 4–6.

Harbour House, Annapolis

On the city dock, this excellent steak and seafood restaurant is open Monday through Saturday from 11:00 A.M. to 10:00 P.M.; Sunday hours, noon to 10:00 P.M. Open for lunch and dinner, reservations not accepted. In mid-June, the Annual Annapolis Fine Arts Festival is held on the dock in front of the restaurant. Painting by Kenneth Harris.

Crab Imperial
3 pounds crabmeat
4 tablespoons butter
4 tablespoons flour
1³/₄ cup milk
1 teaspoon salt
¹/₂ teaspoon monosodium glutamate
¹/₂ teaspoon dry mustard
2 teaspoons lemon juice
2 teaspoons green pepper, chopped
¹/₂ teaspoon Worcestershire sauce
1 teaspoon onion, chopped

pinch of mace
2 eggs
mayonnaise
paprika

Melt butter in saucepan, stir in flour, add milk, and cook over low heat until thick. Add remaining ingredients, except crabmeat and eggs. Remove from heat and stir in beaten eggs, then gently fold in crabmeat. Place mixture in clam shells, brush with mayonnaise and sprinkle with paprika. Bake in 350° oven for 20 minutes or until hot and brownness is attained. Serves 6–8.

Mrs. K's Toll House, Silver Spring

The guest register here is crowded with the names of senators, congressmen, ambassadors and famous personalities from every walk of life. A delightful country inn just a half-hour from the White House, it is at 9201 Colesville Road (U.S. 29) in Silver Spring. Open noon to 2:30 P.M. and 5:00 to 8:30 P.M. every day except Sunday, when it is open noon to 8:30 P.M. Closed on Monday. Reservations advisable. Painting by John L. Heinly.

Concord Grape Pie

2   quarts Concord grapes
½ cup sugar
½ tablespoon cornstarch
1   tablespoon butter, melted
pastry for two 9-inch crusts

Wash grapes thoroughly (as skins are to be used). Remove skins from grapes. Heat pulp and strain through colander to remove seeds. Mix sugar and cornstarch with a little cold water, then add to pulp along with skins. Add butter and stir mixture well. Pour into lower crust and then top with crust, making slits for steam. (Be sure pie pan is perforated to permit proper baking of lower crust.) Bake in 450° oven for 10 minutes, then in 350° oven for another 35 to 45 minutes. Cool. Delicious served à la mode.

Lee's Inn and Motel, Highlands

This magnificent old inn in the Blue Ridge Mountains was established in 1870 and still retains its original charm, but with all modern conveniences. On a six-acre site, it is surrounded by a number of attractive new cottages which overlook the town of Highlands, the highest incorporated town in eastern America. Breakfast, lunch, and dinner served daily in the Rhododendron Room. There are overnight accommodations and excellent recreation facilities, including a special recreation program for guests' children, supervised by trained counselors. Open May 15 to November 1. Painting by Robert Curran.

Pork Chops, Southern
- 6 center-cut loin pork chops, cut 1¼ inches thick
- 6 large slices onion, cut ¼ inch thick
- 6 large slices tomato, cut ¼ inch thick
- salt
- 6 large green pepper slices, cut 1 inch thick
- 3 cups cooked flaky dry rice

On a grill or frying pan, brown pork chops on both sides for 10 minutes on high heat. Place chops in a 3-inch-deep baking pan. Cover each chop with onion slice, then a tomato slice, sprinkle well with salt. Put cleaned pepper ring around onion and tomato slice, stuff pepper ring with cooked rice. Pour 2 cups water into pan, cover with aluminum foil. Bake in 300° oven for 3½ hours. Baste every 1½ hours with pan drippings, covering rice well. Serves 6.

The Colonial Inn, Hillsborough

Dating from pre-Revolutionary days, this friendly, comfortable inn still offers relaxation and traditional Old South cooking. Owned by Mr. and Mrs. Charles Crawford, Jr., it is open for breakfast, lunch and dinner every day; reservations advisable on Sunday. The address is 153 W. King Street, a mile north of I-85 in Hillsborough, which is ten miles northwest of Durham. Painting by Joseph Cox.

Baked Carolina Country Ham

Put a 15-20-pound country cured ham in a large pot and cover with water. Into water put 1 cup sugar and 1 cup vinegar. Combine 6 peppercorns, 6 allspice berries, 1 pod red pepper and 6 whole cloves in a cloth bag, tied securely. Boil rapidly with ham for 1 hour. Then add 1 additional cup of sugar and 1 cup vinegar. Boil until ham is tender when pierced with fork, about 1¹/₂ hours. Remove from water, and skin. Place ham in large broiling pan, score with fat side up and cover with 1 quart crushed spiced crab apples. Bake 45 minutes at 350°, basting 3-4 times with syrup from apples.

Cornwallis Yams

Boil 6 medium sweet potatoes, peel and mash with potato masher or ricer. Season with ¹/₂ teaspoon salt, ¹/₂ teaspoon cinnamon, ¹/₂ teaspoon nutmeg and ¹/₄ pound butter. Add 3 beaten eggs, ¹/₂ cup grated coconut, ¹/₂ cup crushed pineapple and 1¹/₂ cups milk. Place in greased casserole and top with marshmallows and bake in 350° oven until light brown.

Tony's Sanitary Fish Market & Restaurant, Morehead City

Extending out over Bogue Sound near Atlantic Beach in Morehead City, this restaurant with its large picture windows offers customers a perfect view of fishing boats and pleasure craft wending their way up and down the still waters of the Sound. As the name suggests, the restaurant developed from owner Tony Seamon's fishing boats and market. Open daily from 11:00 A.M. to 8:30 P.M.; closed December 15 to February 1. The address is 501 Evans Street. Painting by C. R. McNeil.

Boque Sound Clam Chowder
1   quart clams
1¹/₃ cups onion, chopped
¹/₃   cup salt pork or bacon fat
3   cups potatoes, diced
salt and white pepper, to taste

Clean and chop clams to desired size. Add onion to clams. Cover with water (or clam juice), add fat drippings or cubed pork and cook 30 minutes, or until tender. Then add potatoes; let come to boil. Cook until potatoes are creamy. Season to taste. Serves 6.

Tarheel Hush Puppies
Stir together: 1 pound fine white corn meal; 1 egg; 1 tablespoon salt; 1 tablespoon sugar; pinch of soda; 1 cup buttermilk. Add water to make a thick consistency. Drop by spoonfuls into 375° oil; cook until crisp and golden. Remove with slotted spoon and drain. Serve with fish. Serves 6.

Berry's On-the-Hill, Orangeburg

This delightful establishment was started as a small business over twenty years ago, but became so popular that owners, Mr. and Mrs. C. C. Berry, Jr., built a larger new building on U.S. Highways 301-601 in the center of Orangeburg. All pastries and bread are baked in their own kitchen. Open every day 6:00 A.M. to 10:00 P.M.; closed December 25 and 26, and the week of July 4. Painting by Joseph Cox.

Chocolate Cream Pie

2 egg whites
1/8 teaspoon salt
1/8 teaspoon cream of tartar
1/2 cup sugar
1/2 cup pecans, chopped
1 1/2 teaspoons vanilla
1/4 pound semisweet chocolate
1 1/2 tablespoons powdered sugar
2 cups whipping cream, whipped

Beat egg whites until foamy, add salt and cream of tartar. Beat until mixture stands in soft peaks. Add sugar gradually, beat until very stiff. Fold in chopped pecans and 1/2 teaspoon vanilla. Turn into lightly greased 8-inch pie plate. Hake a nestlike shell, building up side above edge of plate. Bake in 300° oven for 35 minutes. Cool. Melt chocolate in double boiler; add 1 1/2 tablespoons powdered sugar with 3 tablespoons hot water, blend. Cool. Add 1 teaspoon vanilla. Fold in half of whipped cream. Turn into meringue shell, chill. When ready to serve, cover top with rest of whipped cream. Serves 6.

Little Greenbrier Lodge, near Gatlinburg

A perfect vacation spot for people who want to "get away from it all" is this charming rustic lodge just outside the Great Smoky Mountains National Park. Open from first of June into November. Meals served to guests only; reservations necessary. The lodge is 13 miles west of Gatlinburg, a mile and a half off State Highway 73. Painting by Richard Brough.

Individual Chocolate Pies

2 tablespoons flour
1 cup sugar
2 egg yolks, well beaten
2 squares unsweetened chocolate, melted
1 teaspoon butter
pinch of salt
1 teaspoon vanilla
1 cup whipping cream, whipped
8 flaky pastry shells, baked and cooled

Mix flour with sugar, add beaten yolks and melted chocolate. Mix well and put in double boiler and add 1 cup boiling water, mixing thoroughly. Stir mixture constantly over boiling water until it thickens. When done, take off heat and add butter, salt, and vanilla. Beat long and hard. Chill. Pour chocolate filling into shells and top with sweetened whipped cream; sprinkle with nutmeg.

Regas Restaurant, Knoxville

For 47 years the Regas family has operated this restaurant at 318 N. Gay Street at Magnolia Avenue in downtown Knoxville — just off Interstate Highway 40. Lunch and dinner served daily 10:30 A.M. to midnight. Closed only Christmas Eve and Christmas Day. Painting by Douglas Grant.

German Chocolate Cake
- ½ cup pure butter
- 2 cups granulated sugar
- ½ cup vegetable shortening
- 4 eggs
- 1 teaspoon soda
- ¼ teaspoon salt
- 2½ cups plain flour
- 4 tablespoons cocoa
- 1 cup buttermilk
- 4 tablespoons cold black coffee
- 1 teaspoon vanilla

Cream butter, shortening and sugar together, then add eggs one at a time. Sift all dry ingredients together. Add to the creamed mixture alternately with the buttermilk, half at a time. Finally, add coffee and vanilla. Bake in three 9-inch layers for 35 minutes in a 350° preheated oven.

Filling and Icing
- 1 cup cream
- 1 cup sugar
- 3 egg yolks
- 1 teaspoon vanilla
- ¼ pound butter
- 1 cup coconut
- 1 cup pecans, chopped

Place cream, sugar, egg yolks, vanilla and butter in saucepan, and cook together 10 minutes, stirring all the time. Add coconut and pecans. Cool and spread on cool cake.

Justine's, Memphis

Housed in a charming old plantation house of French Provincial style, this restaurant is celebrated among Memphis residents and visitors because of its French cuisine. Just a few blocks west of the intersection of U.S. Highways 78 and 51 (919 Coward Place), it is not marked by any commercial sign, but gourmets know it well. Dinner is served daily from 5:00 P.M. to 10:00 P.M. in the opulent dining room, and, weather permitting, in the garden patio; reservations necessary. Closed Sunday and Christmas Day. Dayton and Justine Smith are the owners. Painting by Billy Price Hosmer.

Lotus Ice Cream

2¹/₃ quarts light cream
3   cups sugar
grated rind of 5 lemons
¹/₄   cup toasted almonds, chopped
2   teaspoons almond extract
1   cup lemon juice

Combine ingredients in order listed and mix well together. Freeze either by hand or electric freezer, or by the refrigerator method. Makes about 4 quarts of ice cream. A refreshing and unusual dessert for a holiday party.

Pappy's Lobster Shack, Memphis

Accompanying the two-pound lobsters, T-bones, and such southern delicacies as ham with red-eye gravy and Tennessee catfish, is the specialty of the house, "Pappy's Southern Rolls," named after L. C. "Pappy" Sammons, who owns and operates the Shack. Located at 2100 Madison Avenue, the restaurant is open seven days a week for lunch and dinner. Painting by Dolph Smith III.

Pappy's Southern Rolls

1 yeast cake, or 1 envelope dry yeast
1/3 cup lukewarm water
3 eggs
1/2 cup shortening, melted
1/3 cup milk, room temperature
1 tablespoon sugar
1 teaspoon salt
3 cups sifted all-purpose flour
1/4 pound butter or margarine

Dissolve yeast in water for 10 minutes. Drop eggs into mixing bowl, add melted shortening, milk, dissolved yeast, sugar and salt. Beat well and begin working in the flour. Knead continuously in the bowl until it's a good dough, smooth and elastic. Cover and let rest in warm place 45 minutes or until double in bulk. Punch down dough. Cut off small pieces about the size of a walnut. Place pieces in greased muffin tins. Let rise in a warm place until roll is high as the pan. Then bake in a 400° oven for 8-12 minutes. When hot from oven brush with butter to give extra flavor. Makes 2 dozen rolls.

Al Sullivan's Restaurant, Murfreesboro

There are four dining rooms at this restaurant on U.S. Highways 41 and 70S in Murfreesboro, Tennessee (32 miles southeast of Nashville). A coffee shop offers quick and inexpensive service for the motorist in a hurry, and there are three other dining rooms which offer full-course dinners. Located in an area rich in recreational and historic attractions. Al Sullivan's Restaurant is connected to a 70-unit motel. Open for breakfast, lunch and dinner every day. Reservations necessary for overnight accommodations. Painting by Frances M. Stephenson.

Shrimp Crabmeat au Gratin
4   ounces steamed crabmeat
4   ounces cooked shrimp
3   ounces boiled codfish
1   green pepper, chopped fine
$^1/_2$ onion, chopped fine
1   stalk celery, chopped fine
3   tablespoons margarine
1   pint cream sauce
$^1/_2$ cup white wine
1   teaspoon lemon juice
2   teaspoons minced pimento

6   ounces grated American
    cheese

Combine crabmeat, shrimp, and codfish. Fry green pepper, onion and celery in margarine for about 10 minutes and let cool, then mix vegetables and seafood. Add cream sauce, wine, lemon juice and pimentos; put ingredients in 6-8 seashells or individual ramekins. Top with grated cheese. Bake for 10 minutes. Serves 6–8.

Miss Martha's Restaurant, Nashville

This dining room of the Allen Hotel at 2004 West End Avenue in downtown Nashville is within walking distance of Centennial Park where visitors may see an exact replica of the Parthenon in Athens. H. J. Allen is always on hand to greet guests for breakfast, lunch, or dinner. Closed last week of December and first week in January. Painting by Bill Gronstaff.

Eggbread
2 cups cornmeal
1/2 teaspoon salt
1 level teaspoon baking powder
1/2 teaspoon soda
2 cups buttermilk
2 eggs
1/3 cup lard, melted

Sift meal, add salt and baking powder. Dissolve soda in buttermilk and stir into mixture. Beat eggs and combine with melted lard, then blend thoroughly into batter. Stir well and spread 1/2 inch thick in 8 x 12 preheated greased pan. Bake in 425° oven for 25 minutes or until brown.

Hostess Salad Dressing
Combine: 1 tablespoon green onions, chopped; 1 cup mayonnaise; 1/4 teaspoon garlic, chopped; 1 teaspoon parsley, chopped; 1 pint yogurt or sour cream; 1/2 pound bleu cheese, crumbled; 1 teaspoon anchovy paste; 3 drops Tabasco sauce; 1/8 teaspoon red pepper; 3 tablespoons lemon juice. Stir well. Store in refrigerator.

The Saddle Restaurant, Shelbyville

This fine restaurant, owned by Mr. and Mrs. George Frey, is at 713 North Main Street (intersection of U.S. 231 and U.S. 41A) in Shelbyville. The menu features southern regional dishes. Open every day except Monday, for lunch and dinner. Closed first two weeks in October. Painting by Paul Brewer.

Rum Cream Pie

Make a crumb pie shell in a 9-inch pie pan. Beat 6 egg yolks until light, add 1 cup sugar. Soak 1 envelope gelatin in 1/2 cup cold water. Bring gelatin and water to a boil and pour over egg mixture. Whip 1 pint whipping cream until stiff, fold it into egg mixture and flavor with 1/2 cup dark rum. Cool until mixture begins to set, pour it into pie shell, chill until firm. Sprinkle top of pie with shaved bittersweet chocolate curls or chopped nuts. Garnish with whipped cream. Serves 8

Roast Sirloin of Beef Frances

Rub 8-10-pound sirloin roast with 1/2 cup salt and pepper. Combine following ingredients: 1/4 cup claret; 1/4 cup wine vinegar; 1/4 cup Worcestershire sauce; 1/4 cup monosodium glutamate; 1 tablespoon garlic powder or garlic clove; 2 tablespoons onion powder; pinch of rosemary, bay leaf, oregano and marjoram; 2 each: sliced carrots, celery stalks and onions. Pour this marinade on roast and keep in cool place for a few hours. Pour off marinade. Roast at 300° until 140° is reached on a meat thermometer for a rare roast.

Battletown Inn, Berryville

This pleasant country inn is at 102 West Main Street (State Highway 7) in Berryville, which is about 60 miles west of Washington, D.C. Open weekdays from 11:00 A.M. to 8:30 P.M.; Sunday closing time is 7:00 P.M. Closed on Mondays and from December 23 to March 8. Mary Murray and her family are the owners. Painting by John Heinly.

Baked Squash

7 small yellow summer squash
1/2 cup cream
1/4 cup saltine crackers, crushed
1 small onion, diced
2 tablespoons butter

Slice squash, then boil in salted water until done. Drain and mash. Sauté onion in 2 tablespoons butter. Add cream, crackers and onion to squash. Pour into greased casserole and top with butter dots and a few breadcrumbs. Bake at 400°, about 1/2 hour or until firm. Serves 10–12.

The Mimslyn, Luray

Spring and summer are particularly beautiful in the area surrounding this delightful inn on U.S. 211 overlooking Skyline Drive in Shenandoah National Park. The green mountains glow with dogwood and laurel, and it is an ideal time to enjoy hiking, golf, tennis and swimming. Breakfast, lunch and dinner served daily. Overnight accommodations; reservations advisable. Painting by Julia Bristow.

Shenandoah Apple Pie
Combine: 3 cups thickly sliced apples, 1 cup grated cheddar-type cheese, 1 cup sugar, 1 tablespoon flour, 1 tablespoon melted butter, 1/2 teaspoon nutmeg and 1/2 teaspoon cinnamon. Fill a 9-inch pastry shell with the apple mixture and cover with top crust. Bake in 350° oven for 45 minutes.

Hot Cakes
Combine: 1 egg, 1 cup milk and 2 tablespoons melted shortening. Then add 1 1/2 cups flour, 1/4 teaspoon salt, 3 1/2 teaspoons baking powder and 1 tablespoon sugar; beat until smooth. Pour generous portions on lightly greased griddle. Yields 16 six-inch pancakes. Serve with maple syrup.

The Captain's Grill, Richmond

In the John Marshall Hotel at 6th and Franklin streets in Richmond, the Grill has the warm, robust décor of an old English inn. Desserts, salads, and flambés are brought on carts and served with a flourish by the headwaiter. Open daily noon to midnight. Reservations advisable. Painting by Kenneth Harris.

Treasures of the Sea
1 cup cooked lobster meat, diced
1 cup cooked crabmeat
1 cup cooked shrimp
1 cup mayonnaise
2 tablespoons chili sauce
1 hard-boiled egg, chopped
1/2 teaspoon salt
1 tablespoon lemon juice
2 tablespoons chopped sweet
   pickles
lettuce
1 tablespoon capers

To make sauce, blend together mayonnaise, chili sauce, chopped hard-boiled egg, salt, lemon juice and chopped sweet pickles. Combine sauce with mixture of seafood. Serve on lettuce leaf. Sprinkle capers on top of seafood. Serves 5.

Fruit of the Sea, Old English Style
Mix 1 egg with 1 cup milk. Sprinkle salt on 12 shrimp, roll in flour. Dip shrimp in egg-milk mixture and then in breadcrumbs. Prepare 12 scallops, 12 oysters, and 6 pieces fillet of sole (3 inches long) in same manner as shrimp. Deep-fry all seafood at 360°. Split 6 lobster tails and broil. Serve all together. Serves 6.

Grapetree Bay Hotel, St. Croix, Virgin Islands

Here is a spot of perfect harmony between luxurious shore living and the Caribbean Sea at the eastern end of St. Croix. John and Lee Burgess welcome vacationers at this modified American-plan resort. Closed during September and October. Meal reservations necessary for nonguests. Mail address: Box P, Christiansted, St. Croix, Virgin Islands. Painting by George Yater.

Cruzan Potatoes

1/2 cup butter
1 cup chopped onions
1 cup chopped sweet green peppers
1 cup chopped celery
1 cup raisins
2 tablespoons thyme
1 small can tomato paste
1 tablespoon Tabasco
6 eggs
6 cups mashed potatoes
(instant potatoes may be used)

For 10 minutes sauté in butter the onions, peppers, celery, raisins and spices, well mixed with the tomato paste. Beat eggs and mix well with potatoes. Combine both mixtures and bake in 350° oven for 25-30 minutes until firm. Serves 8.

Illinois

Indiana

Iowa

Michigan

Minnesota

Nebraska

North Dakota

Ohio

South Dakota

Wisconsin

Here the traveler enjoys a double treat. His eye can feast on the beauty of orchards in bloom, rolling fields of grain, dairy herds roaming the meadows, and lakes that abound with fish. Also, in this region's hospitable homes and restaurants, he may dine on such varied fare as Watercress Soup, Pheasant with Wild Rice, Old-fashioned Applesauce Cake, Charcoal-Broiled Pork Chops, and Swiss Fondue. It's a pleasant land to travel.

NORTH
CENTRAL

Simonini's, Algonquin

Since 1921 the Simonini family has operated this friendly restaurant at the junction of Illinois highways 31 and 62 in Algonquin (about a 45-minute drive northwest of the Chicago Loop). Italian and American cuisine featured. Open Tuesday through Sunday for lunch and dinner; dinner only served on Monday. Closed most holidays. Reservations required on weekends. Painting by Ray Naylor.

Watercress Soup

In 3 tablespoons of butter sauté together: 1 cup celery, diced, 1 cup chopped white onion, and finely diced stems from 2 bunches of watercress. Add 4 cups chicken broth and simmer until celery is tender. Season to taste with salt and pepper. Add watercress leaves to broth. Simmer for 2 minutes. Stir in 2 eggs until they separate into shreds. Serve with toasted French bread sprinkled with Parmesan cheese. Serves 5.

Veal Scaloppine Marsala

Cut 1$\frac{1}{4}$ pounds thinly sliced veal steak into 2-inch squares. Flatten out. Roll in $\frac{1}{4}$ cup flour seasoned with salt and pepper. Heat 4 tablespoons butter in a skillet, then brown meat in butter until almost done. Add 4 tablespoons minced onion, 2 cloves, minced garlic and $\frac{1}{4}$ pound fresh mushrooms (or 8-ounce can) and cook gently. Then add 4 tablespoons Marsala, 1 teaspoon minced parsley, and $\frac{1}{4}$ cup meat stock. Simmer 15 minutes. Serve hot. Serves 5.

Kungsholm, Chicago

Famous for its excellent Scandinavian cuisine and world-famous Miniature Grand Opera, this Chicago restaurant is at 100 E. Ontario, just off Michigan Avenue. Luncheon and dinner guests enjoy two hours of entertainment at no extra charge. In a separate opera theater, accommodating 208 people, guests watch puppets perform in such opera classics as Tosca, La Bohème, Carmen or highlights from Broadway musicals. Closed on Mondays. Kungsholm is open 11:30 A.M. to 10:30 P.M.; Sunday 12:30 to 10:00 P.M. Painting by Paul Brewer.

Danish Roast Leg of Lamb

Make about 6 slits in a 6-8-pound leg of lamb. Stuff slits with $1/2$ pound of salt pork cut into small pieces, and whole parsley sprigs. Roast meat in 325° oven for 3-4 hours for medium. Cook 2 small heads of cauliflower and 16 asparagus spears to desired tenderness. Boil and peel 1 pound small red potatoes. Brown 2 tablespoons sugar in a heavy skillet, then add $1/4$ pound butter and blend. Add potatoes, turning carefully until each is glazed. Place roast on large platter, surround with cauliflower and asparagus topped with 1 cup of Hollandaise sauce and glazed potatoes. Serves 4-6.

The Cellar, Geneseo

The glass-enclosed kitchen with its large charcoal grills is the focal point of this restaurant in the Hotel Geneseo at 137 South State Street in downtown Geneseo (one mile north of Interstate 80). Robert and Stanley Bestor, who own the hotel, pride themselves on their restaurant's cuisine which features premium quality foods, simply prepared. Dinner served 5:00 P.M. to 10:00 P.M. daily; Sunday noon to 10:00 P.M. Reservations advisable on the weekends. Overnight accommodations. Painting by L. A. Horney.

Charcoal-Broiled Shrimp
45 large shrimp (about 3 pounds 15-count shrimp), uncooked, peeled and deveined

Continental Coffee Company's All Purpose Seasoning, to taste (combination of paprika, salt and monosodium glutamate).

drawn butter and 6 lemon halves

Start charcoal fire and get coals to white heat. For each serving place 7 shrimp on skewer. Season lightly with All Purpose Seasoning. Place on flat grill about 6-8 inches above charcoal. Broil about 3 minutes on each side. Baste with barbecue sauce and keep turning and basting for another 6 minutes, or until done. Remove from skewer. Serve with drawn butter and lemon. Serves 6.

Barbecue Sauce
Combine 13 ounces of Open Pit Barbecue Sauce with 2 ounces melted butter and ¾ teaspoon liquid smoke.

Shady Lane Farm, Marengo

The excellent dining facilities here are combined with a summer stock playhouse, and you can also browse at the P.P. & D. (Poke Peek & Drool) Shops where you will find everything from antique furniture to homemade preserves. Located on U.S. 20, 3 miles west of Marengo, Illinois, Shady Lane is open for lunch and dinner every day except Monday. Reservations advisable. Painting by Frank Beatty.

Chicken Marengo

3½-pound chicken, cut in serving
    pieces
chicken fat or oil
salt and garlic powder, to taste
¼ teaspoon each: thyme and
    pepper
6   medium green onions, sliced
¼ cup black olives, sliced
1½ cups chicken broth
¾ cup sauterne
3   tablespoons tomato paste
1   tablespoon flour

Fry chicken pieces golden brown on both sides in fat or oil. Season with salt, pepper, thyme and garlic powder. Transfer to baking dish. Sprinkle with sliced onions and black olives. Add ½ cup of chicken broth. Bake, uncovered, at 325° for 30 minutes. Add ½ cup of wine combined with tomato paste, cover and bake for 20 minutes or longer. Uncover, bake 10 more minutes. Remove chicken pieces and add remaining wine and broth, with flour, to the sauce. Cook until thickened. Pour hot sauce over chicken and serve. Serves 4.

Bob Hadley's Trolley Bar Steak House, Fort Wayne

Diners have their choice of three dining rooms at this popular restaurant at Calhoun and Superior streets in downtown Fort Wayne. The menu includes such favorites as Alaska king crab, family-style chicken, and broiled steaks and chops. Open every weekday from 10:00 A.M. to 2:00 A.M.; closed on Sunday. Entertainment in the evening. Painting by Norbert Smith.

Italian Chicken Soup
3 quarts rich chicken stock
$\frac{1}{2}$ cup celery, chopped
$\frac{1}{2}$ cup onion, chopped
$\frac{1}{4}$ cup carrot, chopped
pinch of oregano
1 cup cooked chicken, chopped
$\frac{1}{2}$ pound fresh endive, cut up
salt to taste

2 eggs
$\frac{3}{4}$ cup Parmesan cheese, grated
Bring chicken stock to boiling point, add celery, onion, carrot and oregano. Cook for 15 minutes, then add endive and simmer for 10 minutes. Whip eggs with grated cheese and add to soup. Simmer for 15 minutes, or until done. Serves 6.

Glendale House, Indianapolis

There are three dining areas here: a cafeteria, a quick-service dining room and a third that features meals served in leisurely elegance. On the northeast side of Indianapolis, it is south of State Highway 100 at 6101 North Keystone Avenue in the Glendale Shopping Center. Meals served from 11:00 A.M. to 8:00 P.M. in the cafeteria; in the dining rooms 11:00 A.M. to 10:00 P.M. Painting by Edwin Fulwider.

Glendale House Fried Chicken
Split a 2¼-pound fryer into 8 pieces and place in a pot. Cover with water seasoned with 1 teaspoon salt, ½ teaspoon white pepper and ½ teaspoon monosodium glutamate. Bring to a boil. Simmer for about 30 minutes until chicken is about half cooked. Then remove from fire but leave it in cooking water. Cool at room temperature, then place in refrigerator for 24 hours. Remove from gelatinized broth, dip in beaten egg and roll in cracker meal. Deep fry for about 8 minutes at 350°.

Serve immediately with peach slices as garnish. This method allows the full flavor to be retained and reduces frying time.

Grilled Reuben Sandwich
Spread Thousand Island Dressing on slice of light rye bread. Add generous layers of corned beef, Swiss cheese and sauerkraut. Top sandwich with second slice of rye bread. Grill on both sides in butter. Make two off-center cuts and garnish with dill-pickle wedges. Serve hot.

L. S. Ayres Tea Room, Indianapolis

Well known throughout the state as a delightful luncheon spot, the Tea Room is on the eighth floor of the L. S. Ayres store at 1 West Washington Street. Lunch is served from 11:00 A.M. to 3:00 P.M., with store models displaying the latest fashions. Candlelight tea served from 3:00 to 4:30 P.M. Dinner on Thursday evenings only, from 4:30 to 7:00 P.M. Closed Sundays. Painting by Edwin Fulwider.

Canadian Cheese Soup
1/4 cup butter
1/2 cup onions, minced
1/4 cup flour
1 1/2 tablespoons cornstarch
1 quart milk
1 quart stock
1/8 teaspoon soda
1/2 cup carrots, diced
1/2 cup celery, diced
1/6 teaspoon paprika

salt to taste
1 cup rarebit cheese or Old English cheese (cut in small cubes)
2 tablespoons parsley, chopped

Melt butter and sauté onions lightly. Add flour and cornstarch. Blend milk and stock, stirring to make a smooth white sauce. Add soda, vegetables, seasonings, and cheese. Simmer for 15 minutes. Just before serving, add parsley. Makes 2 quarts.

Strongbow Turkey Inn and Farm, Valparaiso

In the center of a turkey farm, this inn features many turkey specialties, all from its own flocks. Packaged gift turkeys and frozen foods are available for shipment, and visitors may also purchase turkey sandwiches for en route lunches. Open every day from 11:00 A.M. to 9:00 P.M.; reservations advisable on Sunday and holidays. Eight miles south of the Indiana Toll Road, Valparaiso exit, this restaurant is on U.S. 30 East, just outside the city limits of Valparaiso. Painting by Norbert Smith.

Strongbow Turkey Salad

Cut 1 pound breast meat of turkey into ¹/₂-inch cubes and combine with ¹/₂ pound of celery chopped medium fine. Marinate lightly in French Dressing (see recipe below), for at least 1 hour before serving. Place large lettuce nests on four salad plates. Pack ³/₄ cup firmly with turkey salad and turn out on each salad plate. Decorate each with ¹/₂ hard-boiled egg, quartered, and 4 tomato wedges. Tuck parsley in on sides. Top each salad with 1 teaspoon mayonnaise and sprinkle with toasted slivered almonds. Serves 4.

Strongbow French Dressing

Place 1 small clove of garlic, slightly crushed, in a bottle. Add: 1 teaspoon salt, ³/₄ teaspoon freshly ground white pepper, ¹/₄ cup cider vinegar. Let stand or shake until salt dissolves. Add 1 cup pure olive oil. Close bottle and refrigerate.

Honeywell Center, Wabash

An excellent restaurant is one of the many facilities in this elegant community center at 275 West Market Street just west of the business district. Lunch served every weekday; no dinners. Dining rooms closed on Saturday and Sunday except for private parties. Painting by E. Algerd Waitkus.

Breast of Chicken Supreme

3 chicken breasts
1/2 pound butter
1 cup onions, sliced
1/2 cup flour
3 cups chicken stock
1 1/2 cups light cream or half-and-half
1/2 cup sherry
1 cup mushrooms
6 slices of ham, 1/4 inch thick
1 cup raw brown or wild rice

Bone and split chicken breasts; melt butter in skillet. Sauté breasts until a light golden brown. Salt to taste. Remove chicken to hot platter, sauté onions, and remove from butter with slotted spoon to drain. Prepare roux by blending flour into butter until it is a smooth paste. Then add chicken stock and cream, blending to keep smooth. Finally add sherry and mushrooms and cook over low heat for 5 minutes. Place chicken on top of heated ham slices and top with sauce. Serve with rice which has been boiled. Makes 6 portions.

E. ALGERD WAITKUS

Vic's Tally-Ho Restaurant, Des Moines

An attractive restaurant in the Merle Hay Shopping Center, it specializes in American-Italian cuisine as well as charcoal-broiled steaks and chops. Take Merle Hay exit from Interstate 80, then turn left one block to 5601 Douglas Avenue. Open for dinner 5:00 P.M. to 1:00 A.M.; closed Sunday. Painting by Richard Wagner.

Spaghetti and Meatballs

- 1/2 pound ground veal
- 1/2 pound ground pork
- 1 clove garlic, chopped fine
- 2 tablespoons chopped parsley
- 1 teaspoon salt
- 1/4 teaspoon pepper
- 1/2 cup breadcrumbs
- 1/4 cup milk
- 1 egg lightly beaten
- 1/4 cup flour
- 1/4 cup olive oil
- 4 tablepsoons chopped onion
- 1 No. 2 1/2 can Italian tomatoes, peeled
- 1 teaspoon basil
- 3 tablespoons tomato paste
- 1 pound spaghetti
- Parmesan cheese

Combine meat, garlic, parsley, 1/2 teaspoon salt, and 1/4 teaspoon pepper, breadcrumbs, milk and egg. Mix thoroughly and shape into 8 balls. Heat olive oil in frying pan, dredge meatballs in flour and brown on all sides in oil. When meatballs are brown, remove from pan reserving oil. Brown onion in oil in same frying pan until golden. Add tomatoes, basil, rest of salt, dash of pepper and simmer 30 minutes. Blend in tomato paste, return meatballs to pan with sauce and simmer 20 minutes longer. While sauce is cooking, cook spaghetti in boiling water until tender, drain and place in serving dish. Pour sauce over spaghetti, mix lightly. Arrange meatballs on top and serve with sprinkling of grated Parmesan cheese. Serves 4.

Steak De Burgo

Butterfly two 7-ounce pieces of choice beef tenderloin. Sauté in garlic butter to desired degree. Sprinkle with chopped parsley and serve immediately. Mushrooms may be used for garnish if desired. Serves 2.

Tallcorn Motor Hotel, Marshalltown

Tom Connelly is the manager of this modern motor hotel and restaurant at 2nd Avenue and Main Street. It is one block west of State Highway 14 and one mile from U.S. Highway 30. Breakfast, lunch and dinner served every day, year around. Overnight accommodations; reservations not necessary. Painting by Richard Wagner.

Peanut Butter Ice Cream Pie
Line a 9-inch pie pan with graham-cracker crust. Thaw out 1 quart of vanilla ice cream, put in mixing bowl with 1 cup of peanut butter and mix thoroughly. Fill crust with mixture and freeze. Serve frozen. Serves 8.

Broiled Live Lobster
Remove claws from lobster, then split lobster in half. Crack meaty parts of claws. Put in small pan, cover with $1/2$ cup of olive oil, sprinkle with paprika and salt. Broil for 15 minutes for $1^1/2$-pound lobster. Serve with lemon wedges and hot butter.

Shanty Creek Lodge, Bellaire

Full year-around vacation facilities and activities make this an excellent family resort. In the winter there are slopes and chairlifts for skiing, and sleigh rides; in other seasons there are spring cherry blossom and autumn foliage tours, swimming in the heated pool, horseback riding, and pond and stream fishing. The lodge is in the northwestern part of the state, 12 miles west of U.S. 131, just off State Highway 88 at Bellaire. Open year around; reservations necessary for overnight accommodations. Breakfast, lunch and dinner served daily. Painting by Rodolphe LaRiviere.

Tomato Pudding
- 1 cup tomato puree
- 1 cup tomato juice
- 1 cup brown sugar
- 8 slices day-old bread with crusts trimmed
- 1/2 cup butter, melted

Combine tomato puree, juice and brown sugar, bring to boil and simmer 10 minutes. Cut bread into squares and dip each piece of bread in melted butter, then place in baking dish. Pour tomato mixture over bread squares. *Do not stir.* Push down lightly with fork until bread is just coated. Bake in 350° oven for 25 minutes. Serve hot with main course. Excellent with both red and white meats. Yields 4 portions.

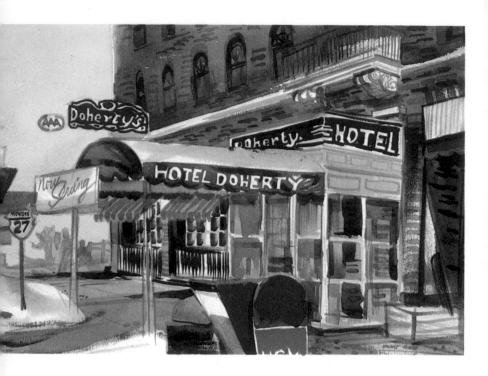

Doherty Motor Hotel, Clare

Tourists bound for a vacation in northern Michigan can spend a night at the Doherty, enjoy the recreational facilities of the hotel, and eat breakfast, lunch and dinner in its dining rooms: open from 7:00 A.M. to 10:30 P.M.; Sunday 8:00 A.M. to 8:45 P.M. The restaurant is at 604 McEwan Street, at junction of U.S. 27 and U.S. 10. Painting by Stuart Hodge.

Hawaiian Chocolate Pie

1 cup sugar
5 tablespoons cornstarch
1/2 cup corn syrup
4 egg yolks
1 teaspoon vanilla
1/2 teaspoon salt
1 cup milk
4 ounces bitter chocolate, melted
1 No. 2 can crushed pineapple, drained
1 cup pecans
1 cup whipping cream, sweetened and whipped
1 9-inch baked pie shell

Combine sugar, cornstarch, corn syrup, egg yolks, vanilla, and salt with milk. Bring mixture to boiling point in a double boiler, stirring constantly. When mixture thickens separate into 2 equal parts. To 1 part add chocolate, to other add drained pineapple. Cover both mixtures and let cool. When cool, put pecans into pie shell and then a thin layer of chocolate filling. Let stand 1 hour, covered. Then add pineapple filling, let stand covered for 1 hour. Add remaining chocolate and chill 2 hours. Then top with whipped cream.

Dearborn Inn and Motor House, Dearborn

Henry Ford had several things in mind when he built the Dearborn Inn, located at 20301 Oakwood Boulevard. It was to be an example of a modern motor inn, providing accommodations and free parking for tourists visiting Greenfield Village and the surrounding area, and it was also to serve airline passengers landing at the Ford Airport formerly across from the inn — thus being the world's first "airport hotel." Breakfast, lunch and dinner are served daily. Overnight accommodations available; reservations recommended. Painting by Lou McMurray.

Pineapple Whipped Cream Pie
1 No. 2½ can crushed pineapple
1 cup sugar
pinch of salt
juice of ½ lemon
2 tablespoons cornstarch
1 unbaked pie shell

whipped cream
Cook pineapple with sugar, salt, and lemon juice. Thicken with cornstarch. Pour into unbaked shell and bake for 30 minutes at 375°. Let cool; then serve topped with whipped cream.

Brau Haus, Detroit

Located in an old mansion at 3462 E. Jefferson Avenue near downtown Detroit, this restaurant is noted for its hearty German dishes. Open for lunch and dinner every weekday, and a special Saturday brunch from 11:00 A.M. to 4:00 P.M. Closed on Sunday from May 30 to September 1. Reservations necessary. August and Lucille Lammerding are the owners. Painting by Robert Boston.

Beef Rouladen
2 pounds round steak, sliced thin
mustard for brushing
1 pound bacon, diced
2 onions, chopped fine
2 green peppers, chopped
4 tablespoons oil
$\frac{1}{2}$ pint boiling water
$\frac{1}{2}$ pint sherry
2 tablespoons cornstarch
hot noodles
Ask your butcher to slice the beef for you. Pound slices lightly and brush each piece with mustard. Mix bacon, onions and peppers together and spread mixture on beef slices. Starting at narrow end, roll up the slices of beef and secure with a skewer or a round toothpick. Heat fat and brown rolls well. Add combined boiling water and sherry, cover and bake in 375° oven until tender, about 2 hours. Make up any water lost by cooking. Thicken gravy with mixture of cornstarch and water. Serve with noodles. Serves 4–6.

Caucus Club, Detroit

With chess and checker games on walnut tables and walls lined with books and magazines, this unusual restaurant resembles a well-appointed private club. Lunch and dinner served daily 11:30 A.M. to 1:00 A.M. Entertainment in the evening. Closed Sunday and holidays. Reservations necessary. In the Penobscot Building at 150 W. Congress Street in downtown Detroit. Painting by Lou McMurray.

Brochette of Beef Tenderloin Polynesian

2 pounds beef tenderloin, sliced
$^3/_4$ cup soy sauce
$^1/_4$ cup honey
$^1/_4$ cup sweet sherry
1 teaspoon curry powder
1 teaspoon salt
pinch of cinnamon
pinch of ground clove
1 teaspoon ginger
1 clove garlic, chopped

Marinate sliced beef tenderloin in remaining ingredients 12-24 hours in advance of cooking. Broil beef on skewers with cubes of fresh pineapple. Serve with rice and mushroom caps. Serves 4.

Hotel Pontchartrain, Detroit

The restaurant shown in the painting, Le Cafe, is one of several in this fine, new downtown Detroit hotel. The others are Restaurant La Mediterranee, Salamandre Bar, Place d'Encore, and Cabaret La Boheme, on the 25th floor, commanding a panoramic view of the city and Canada. At Washington Boulevard and Jefferson Avenue. Painting by Robert Boston.

Stuffed Boston Sole
Skin both sides of 6 Boston yellowtail sole weighing 1½ pounds apiece. Cut pocket along backbone. Chop 1 shallot and sauté in 2 tablespoons butter. To this add 2 pounds King crabmeat, broken up with a fork, and 1 tablespoon flour. Cook for 2 minutes. Add 1 cup cream and mix well. Season with salt, white pepper and 4 tablespoons dry white wine. Stuff sole with crab mixture; sprinkle each fish with salt and paprika. Brush with ¼ cup melted butter and bake 20 minutes at 350°. This recipe serves 6.

Tomatoes Oriental
Hollow out 6 fresh tomatoes slightly. In 2 tablespoons of butter sauté 2 tablespoons finely chopped onions until golden brown. Add 2 cups clear chicken broth and 1 cup raw rice. Season with salt, 1 bay leaf and pinch of Spanish saffron. Cover, simmer until liquid is absorbed. Remove bay leaf and stuff tomatoes with rice mixture. Bake in 350° oven for 15 minutes. Makes 6 portions.

Joe Muer's, Detroit

Whitefish from Lake Superior, perch from Lake Ontario, and baby frogs' legs from Michigan ponds are local delicacies and great favorites at this seafood restaurant at the corner of Gratiot and Vernor Highway East. Open Monday, Tuesday, Wednesday, Thursday, 11:00 A.M. to 9:30 P.M.; Friday 11:00 A.M. to 10:00 P.M.; Saturday 5:00 P.M. to 11:00 P.M. Closed Sundays and holidays. There are no reservations. Painting by Edith Obal.

Deviled Crab

2 pounds fresh crabmeat
1¼ pounds 3-day-old bread
5 hard-boiled eggs, chopped
1 heaping tablespoon salt
1 heaping tablespoon dry mustard
1 large onion
1¼ ounces Worcestershire sauce
1¼ ounces vinegar
3 tablespoons mayonnaise

Cut crust from bread, crumble into small bits, and place in mixing bowl. Add the eggs, salt, and dry mustard. Mix well, then add onion (which has been chopped and sautéed in butter) and flavorings and mix well. Add crabmeat. Form into patties and bake in 350° oven for 15 minutes. Makes from 10 to 12 patties; serves 6.

Little Harry's Restaurant, Detroit

Just a few minutes from downtown Detroit, this fine eating place is housed in a lovely old Federal period home and features an interesting collection of photographs of 19th-century Detroit. Lunch and dinner served every weekday; the dining room is open until 1:00 A.M. Closed on Sunday. Reservations necessary. The address is 2681 East Jefferson. Painting by M. Y. Cheng.

Filet of Sole Bonne Femme

2 pounds fillet of sole (or any light-colored fish)
1 lemon (juice only)
3 ounces dry white wine
1 teaspoon thyme
4 bay leaves
12 shucked oysters
6 shrimp, boiled and peeled
salt and freshly ground white pepper, to taste
$1/2$ cup melted butter
$1/2$ cup flour
7 egg yolks

In a shallow pan place fillet of sole, then add lemon juice, wine, seasonings and oysters. Add cold water to cover, about $6^1/2$ cups, and poach for approximately 8 minutes or until fish is cooked. Then strain off fish broth and save 4 cups.

In a separate pan heat butter, slowly add flour and now blend 4 cups of fish broth in mixture. Simmer for 10 minutes and slowly add egg yolks, one at a time, while constantly stirring. Place oysters and shrimp on fish fillets, pour sauce over the fish and bake in a 475° oven until golden brown.

Schweizer's, Detroit

Celebrating its 106th birthday this year, Schweizer's still offers the same kind of hearty German fare that first made it an institution with Detroiters. It is close to the Detroit River and the heart of the city at 260 Schweizer Place. Open for lunch and dinner on weekdays; dinner only on Saturday. Closed on Sunday. Painting by Adele Bichan.

Sauerbraten

Cover a lean, 4-pound piece of beef round in the following mixture: 1 cup of vinegar; 3 cups of water; 2 cloves garlic; 2 sliced onions; 1 cut carrot; salt and pepper to taste; 1 bay leaf and a generous tablespoon pickling spices. Marinate 5 days in refrigerator. Remove meat from the marinade, dust with flour and brown in 3 tablespoons corn oil in oven. When meat is brown, add 1½-2 cups of the marinade (depending on the pan size), the vegetables, 1 teaspoon sugar, and 1 diced tomato. Braise until meat is tender. Strain the sauce left in the pan, thicken with 4 or 5 gingersnaps and correct seasoning. Meat should be sliced thin,

5 or 6 slices per person, topped with the gravy, garnished with potato pancakes.

Potato Pancakes

Grate or grind — never use blender — 4 medium-sized peeled potatoes and 1 small onion into a sieve. Remove as much water as possible. Then transfer to bowl, add three eggs, 1 tablespoon flour, 1 teaspoon baking powder, and ½ teaspoon salt. Gently mix. Fry in ¼-inch hot corn oil. For thick, fluffy pancakes, slide a spoonful of batter gently into the hot oil, heaped high. Turn once. When pancakes are a golden brown, remove and blot. Makes 8 pancakes, serves 4.

Topinka's Country House, Detroit

Consistently good food served with a flair in three beautifully appointed dining rooms have made Ken Nicholson's restaurant a popular suburban stop. At edge of northwest Detroit, on corner of Seven Mile and Telegraph roads (U.S. 24). Open 11:00 A.M. to 2:00 A.M. on weekdays; Sunday 2:00 P.M. to 10:00 P.M. Reservations advisable. Painting by Adele Bichan.

Old-Fashioned Coconut Cake
Batter

2¼ cups sifted all-purpose flour
⅓ cup cornstarch
1 teaspoon baking powder
½ cup butter or margarine
2 cups sugar
¾ cup milk
1 tablespoon vanilla extract
6 egg whites

Start oven at 375°. Grease 3 round 8-inch cake pans: coat with film of flour. Sift flour, cornstarch, and baking powder 3 times. Set aside. Work butter or margarine until soft. Add sugar gradually and continue working until very creamy. Mix milk and vanilla extract. Then stir flour mixture and milk alternately into creamed butter and sugar. Be sure to start and end with flour combination. Beat egg whites until they hold a point; fold into batter; pour into cake pans. Bake 25 minutes, or until cakes pull away slightly from side of pan. Cool about 5 minutes, then remove.

Frosting

Mix 2 egg whites, ¾ cup sugar, 2½ tablespoons cold water, ½ teaspoon cream of tartar, and pinch of salt in top of double boiler. Beat until well mixed. Cook over rapidly boiling water, beating vigorously 7 minutes, until frosting holds definite peaks. Remove from heat and cool. Beat 1 cup heavy cream until it holds a shape. Fold into cold frosting along with 1 teaspoon vanilla and 1 cup of grated coconut. Spread frosting between cake layers and on sides and top. Sprinkle with another cup of coconut.

House of Ludington, Escanaba

In Michigan's Upper Peninsula, this 103-year-old hotel at 223 Ludington Street, overlooking Little Bay de Noc, is famous for its excellent modern facilities and imaginative food. Mr. and Mrs. Henry Ford often stopped here on their way to the Ford properties at Iron Mountain. Open for breakfast, lunch and dinner. Closed on Sunday during winter for dinner. Overnight accommodations, free garage, and recreation facilities. Reservations advisable in the summer. Pat Hayes is the owner-manager. Painting by Arthur J. Barbour.

Cheese Cake

1½ pounds cream cheese, room temperature
4 egg whites
1 cup sugar
1 teaspoon vanilla
⅔ cup zwieback crumbs

Cream the cheese well to soften. Beat egg whites until stiff, add sugar gradually. Blend egg whites and cheese. Add vanilla. Butter an 8-inch by 3-inch-deep spring-form pan. Add crumbs. Bake at 350° for 25 minutes. Then cover with topping.

Topping

Combine 2 cups thick sour cream with 2 tablespoons sugar and 1 teaspoon vanilla. Spread over top of warm cheese cake and sprinkle with ⅓ cup toasted shaved blanched almonds. Bake 5 minutes in 475° oven. Chill 2 hours. If desired, garnish with fresh fruit.

Botsford Inn, Farmington

Henry Ford bought and restored this hostelry, which once served as a stage stop on the line between Detroit and Chicago. Built in 1836, it combines the warm hospitality and charm of a more relaxed era with modern motor hotel accommodations and delicious food. Located at 28000 Grand River in Farmington, the inn is now owned by Anhut Hotels. Breakfast and lunch served every day, except Monday. Dinner served 5:00 P.M. to 10:00 P.M. daily. Room reservations advisable. Painting by Jerold Deagen.

Egg Nog Pie
Place in double boiler: 2 cups milk, 3/4 cup sugar and pinch of salt and cook until hot. Separate 4 eggs and combine yolks with 2 tablespoons cornstarch and beat well. Add yolks to hot milk mixture. Flavor with 3 tablespoons rum. Cook until mixture thickens, stirring occasionally. Just before removing from fire, beat 2 egg whites with 2 tablespoons sugar until stiff. Pour into custard. Pour into 8-inch baked pie shell and chill. Sprinkle with nutmeg and top with whipped cream before serving.

Dutch Oven Chicken
Split 3-pound chicken. Wash and sprinkle with salt and pepper, then dust lightly with flour. Sauté in butter on both sides until golden brown. Place in baking dish and cover thoroughly with your favorite cream sauce. Sprinkle with paprika and bake at 300° for 1 hour. Serves 4.

Frankenmuth Bavarian Inn, Frankenmuth

The Zehnder family, famous in Frankenmuth as restaurant operators, recently built an Old World addition to Fischer's Hotel which includes a large Bavarian dining room, a Kaffee Haus, Tap Room and Sunken Lounge. Open for breakfast, lunch and dinner every day, except Monday. Reservations desirable. It is five miles east of I-75 Expressway; northbound take Birch Run exit, southbound take Bridgeport exit to 713 S. Main Street. The Frankenmuth Bavarian Festival is held in the town the second full week in June. Painting by Rudolph LaRiviere.

Frankenmuth Bean Salad

1 pound Michigan small navy beans
1¼ cups celery, diced
½ cup onions, chopped
½ cup green pepper, chopped
½ cup French dressing
½ cup vinegar
½ cup sugar
1 teaspoon dry mustard
½ teaspoon garlic salt
¼ teaspoon paprika
¾ teaspoon monosodium glutamate
½ teaspoon salt
several pimentos.

Soak beans overnight. Cover beans with water and simmer on top of stove until tender. Drain well and cool. Then add remaining ingredients. Let stand about 4 hours in refrigerator before serving. Serves 10–12.

Inman's, Galesburg

One wall is a giant picture window which allows diners to gaze out on the Kalamazoo River and see swans and geese glide by. It is lighted at night. Atmosphere is not the restaurant's only claim to fame; the owner, Andy Levene, insists that its reputation be built on good food. Lunch and dinner served every day. An appetizer buffet is served noon to midnight; Sunday closing 7:30 P.M. Reservations advisable. On the city limits of Galesburg, it is at 400 E. Michigan. Take Galesburg exit from 1-94 (between Battle Creek and Kalamazoo). Painting by Leontine Wallace.

Steak Tidbits Mignon

Cut 11 ounces of beef tenderloin into 1-inch cubes. Sauté in 2 tablespoons butter in a hot skillet. Season to taste with salt, pepper and garlic. Add ¼ cup diced onions and ½ cup sliced mushrooms. Cook over low heat. Add 2 ounces Bordelaise sauce, either commercially prepared or homemade. Serve immediately. Serves 2.

Win Schuler's Restaurant, Marshall

Win Schuler transformed this small-town hotel restaurant into a world-famous eating place. There are three other Schuler restaurants in Michigan today patterned on the original. Before he orders, each dinner patron is served a heaping basket of garlic toast, a brown crock of special bar cheese, a fresh hot loaf of homemade bread and a fancy relish tray with appetizers. It is one block east of U.S. 27 and one block south of Business Loop 94 at 115 S. Eagle Street in downtown Marshall. Open for Continental breakfast, lunch and dinner. Closed only on Christmas. Overnight accommodations. Painting by Lou McMurray.

Schuler's Grasshopper Pie

Crust

Combine 1¼ cups crushed chocolate cooky wafers with ⅓ cup melted butter. Pat into deep 9-inch pie pan and chill.

Filling

⅔ cup milk, scalded
24 marshmallows
2 ounces green crème de menthe
1 ounce white crème de cacao

½ pint whipping cream, whipped

Add marshmallows to scalded milk in double boiler, stirring often until they blend into smooth mixture. Cool to room temperature. Then add crème de menthe and crème de cacao. Fold whipped cream into mixture and pour into chilled chocolate crust. Freeze a minimum of 2 hours. If frozen overnight, it should be partially thawed before serving. Serves 8.

Old Hickory House, Midland

Guests choose one of the top-choice steaks, which are labeled for weight and price, and this cost includes the entire dinner. The steak is then cooked over a charcoal and hickory-wood fire to individual taste. Open for dinner daily; closed holidays. Reservations appreciated. Owned by Henne Brothers, Old Hickory is at 3626 N. Saginaw Road in Midland. From I-75 take Eastman Road exit south to first traffic light, then drive right one mile. Painting by Stuart Hodge.

Chick-pea Salad
1 quart chick peas, cooked
1 cup vinegar
1/2 cup oil
1 medium onion, chopped
1/2 cup celery, chopped
1/4 cup pimento, chopped
1/4 cup green pepper, chopped
1/2 teaspoon oregano
1/2 teaspoon salt
1/4 teaspoon pepper
1/4 teaspoon ground garlic
Drain chick peas and combine re-maining ingredients into a well-mixed dressing. Add to chick peas and keep refrigerated until serving. May be served as a relish for buffet service. Serves 20.

Sour Cream Dressing
As a dressing for baked potatoes, grind 1 medium onion and 1 table-spoon of parsley together, using finest blade. Combine and mix thoroughly with 1 pint of sour cream and 1 table-spoon salt.

The Embers, Mt. Pleasant

A half-mile west of the U.S. 27 Freeway at 1217 S. Mission Street, this restaurant, near Central Michigan University, is owned by Clarence Tuma. Guests, with the exception of dieters, love the cart heaped with magnificent homemade pastries which comes to each table at the end of the main course. Lunch and dinner served daily; Sunday hours noon to 8:00 P.M. Painting by Grace McArthur.

Charcoal-Broiled Pork Chops Marinade

Mix and bring to a boil: 2 cups soy sauce, 1 cup water, 1/2 cup brown sugar, 1 tablespoon dark molasses and 1 teaspoon salt. Place 6 center-cut pork chops, bone side up, in pan and pour cooled marinade over chops and let stand overnight in refrigerator. Next day place chops in baking pan and cover tight with foil. Place in 375° oven and bake until tender, about 2 hours.

Red Sauce

While chops are baking, combine 1 tablespoon dry mustard, 1/4 cup of water, 1 cup brown sugar, leaving no lumps. Combine with 1 regular size bottle ketchup and 1 bottle chili sauce, place in heavy pan or double boiler and bring to a slight boil. When chops are tender, remove from oven, dip in red sauce and bake for 30 minutes in uncovered pan at 350° until slightly glazed. Keep chops at room temperature until ready to put on charcoal pit. Over small bed of coals raised as high as possible, grill chops up to 15 minutes. Serves 6.

Gull Harbor Inn, Richland

The view from the picture windows at this country inn reveals rolling lawn, magnificent trees and the beauty of Gull Lake. Richland is 15 miles northeast of Kalamazoo (via State Highway 43) and 15 miles northwest of Battle Creek (via State Highway 89); both routes are just north of I-94. Lunch served 11:30 A.M. to 3:00 P.M.; dinner 5:00 P.M. to 11:00 P.M. Sunday hours noon to 8:00 P.M. Closed on Monday. Reservations advisable. Painting by Robert Boston.

Pepper Steak

3 tablespoons butter or olive oil
1 medium onion, cut in large pieces
1 medium green pepper, cut in 1-inch squares
1½ pound sirloin, sliced thin and cut in 2-inch pieces
2 tablespoons flour
½ cup Claret

1 tomato, diced, or 8 cherry tomatoes, halved
8-ounce can sliced mushrooms

Melt butter or oil in skillet and sauté onion and green pepper, covered, for 5 minutes. Season pieces of meat with salt and pepper, roll in flour, add to skillet and brown. Add wine, tomatoes and mushrooms. Finish cooking. Season to taste and serve with potato and salad. Serves 4.

Patterson's Supper Club, Sturgis

About halfway between Detroit and Chicago on U.S. 112, or between Toledo and Chicago via the turnpikes, this restaurant at Sturgis serves good American food for both luncheon and dinner. Leave the Indiana Toll Road at Interchange 9; Sturgis is four miles north across the Michigan state line. Open every day except Monday until 11:00 P.M. The address is 1106 West Chicago Road. Painting by Norbert Smith.

Beefsteak Pie, Country Style
2 pounds round steak, 1-inch cubes
2 tablespoons shortening or beef fat
1 cup onions, sliced
salt, pepper, monosodium glutamate, to taste
1 tablespoon Worcestershire sauce
2 tablespoons parsley, chopped
2 cups potatoes, diced
1 tablespoon butter
2 tablespoons flour
2 cups biscuit dough

Brown round steak pieces in hot fat, then add onion slices seasoned with salt, pepper, monosodium glutamate, Worcestershire sauce, and parsley. Brown lightly. Cover with boiling water and simmer slowly for 30 minutes. Add diced potatoes and cook 45 minutes. Melt butter over low fire and blend flour into it until it is a smooth paste. Add to beef mixture. Stir well. Pour thickened mixture into deep baking dish and cool slightly. Cover with a thin layer of biscuit dough and bake in 400° oven about 12-15 minutes until crust is brown. Serves 4-6.

The London House, Duluth

This restaurant is on U.S. Highway 61, which is the principal highway between Minneapolis-St. Paul and the Canadian border and is part of the new circle route around Lake Superior. Open for lunch and dinner daily 11:00 A.M. to 1:00 A.M.; dinner reservations necessary in the summer. The address is 2502 London Road, 5 minutes from downtown. Painting by Earl Gross.

Crabmeat Remick
4 slices toast
1 pound king crabmeat
8 strips bacon
1½ cups mayonnaise
½ cup chili sauce
½ teaspoon paprika
few drops Tabasco and
    Worcestershire sauce

Place slices of toast in 4 individual casseroles, then top with an equal portion of crab for each. Cut each strip of bacon into 4 pieces and place 8 pieces on each casserole. Bake in hot oven (450°) until bacon is crisp (about 15 minutes). Combine remaining ingredients into sauce and pour over casseroles, then put under broiler, about 10 inches from broiler, until sauce bubbles and is golden brown. Serves 4.

Gaslight, Minneapolis

The romance and atmosphere of the gaslight era pervade this unique Twin City restaurant. Owner Leonard Bonander says, "Fine foods and atmosphere are what we attempt to offer our customers." Situated at 1420 Washington Avenue South, in downtown Minneapolis, it is open for lunch from 11:30 A.M. to 2:30 P.M., for dinner from 5:00 P.M. to 11:45 P.M. Open every day except holidays. Reservations accepted. Painting by Jerome Ryan.

Seafood Newburg

- 4 tablespoons butter
- 1 quart cooked seafood (shrimp, lobster, crabmeat mixed)
- 4 egg yolks
- 2 cups cream
- 4 tablespoons flour
- ½ cup Madeira or sherry
- 1 tablespoon sugar
- 1 tablespoon Worcestershire sauce
- Dash of red pepper or Tabasco sauce
- ½ teaspoon salt
- ½ teaspoon paprika
- toasted bread

Melt butter in skillet. Add seafood and allow to simmer for 5 minutes. In a separate bowl beat egg yolks and add cream previously mixed to a smooth paste with flour. Add wine, sugar, Worcestershire sauce, red pepper, salt and paprika. Stir well. Pour into double boiler and continue cooking until mixture becomes the consistency of thin cream sauce, stirring constantly. Add sauce to seafood and allow to cook for 2 minutes before serving on toasted bread. Serves 6.

Murray's Restaurant, Minneapolis

A specialist in the art of preparing steak, Arthur Murray, owner of this downtown restaurant, advises home chefs "to keep it simple." Diners crowd the dining room here on weekdays from 11:30 A.M. to 1:00 A.M.; dancing 10:15 P.M. to closing time. Closed Sunday. Reservations preferred, especially on weekends. The Tyrone Guthrie Theater is a new attraction nearby. The address is 26 South 6th Street between Nicollet Mall and Hennepin. Painting by Jerome Ryan.

The Thick Steak

Select a frozen New York cut, which most butchers call a club steak, weighing approximately 16 ounces frozen. Put in a 550° oven for 15 minutes to thaw. This will retain the natural flavor of the meat and keep the loss of natural juices to a minimum. Then broil the steak to individual taste. Season with salt, then brush with melted butter, and serve immediately.

The ¾-Inch Steak

Buy a club or T-bone steak approximately ¾-inch thick from your usual market. *Do not broil.* Pan-fry steak in butter, using a very hot fire, 3 minutes on each side. Use salt and pepper to season. Since this type of steak varies in thickness, cooking time will also vary. Pan-frying steaks of this thickness preserves their tenderness and juiciness, whereas broiling will tend to toughen them.

Shakopee House, Shakopee

Established 110 years ago, this charming hostelry is in the heart of the beautiful Minnesota Valley, about 14 miles from the Twin Cities and a block south of U.S. Highways 169 and 212 at 206 Fuller Street. Lunch and dinner served daily; closed Christmas Day. Overnight accommodations. Reservations advisable. Painting by Jerome F. Ryan.

Lobster Polynesian
3 pounds lobster meat
4 tablespoons butter
$^{1}/_{2}$ cup green pepper, chopped
1 tablespoon green onion, chopped
1 cup pimento, chopped
4 water chestnuts, sliced
3 slices pineapple, cubed
$^{1}/_{8}$ teaspoon garlic powder
1 teaspoon Worcestershire sauce
4 teaspoons white vinegar
1 cup pineapple juice
Sauté lobster in butter. Mix in remaining ingredients in a saucepan and cook very slowly. When well cooked, thicken with a little cornstarch mixed with cold water. Put sautéed lobster in a casserole and cover with sauce. Serve Polynesian Rice in a dish on the side. Serves 4.

Polynesian Rice
Simmer together for 5 minutes: 2 cups cooked white rice; $^{1}/_{4}$ cup green pepper, diced; $^{1}/_{4}$ cup pimento, diced; $^{1}/_{2}$ cup mushroom pieces; 1 teaspoon chicken broth. Serves 4.

Flamingo Inn, South Sioux City

Since opening five years ago this restaurant has been famous for its delicious prime ribs of beef, charcoal-broiled steaks, resin-baked potatoes, and salads, all served in a beautiful Old English dining room with two open-hearth char broilers in it. Adjoining is an 80-unit motel, air-conditioned, with king-size beds, heated swimming pool and putting green. It is located at the junction of U.S. Highways 20 and 77 in South Sioux City. Open for breakfast, lunch, dinner and late supper until 2:00 A.M. every day. Reservations advisable. Painting by Robert Amundsen.

Roast Prime Ribs of Beef

In an effort to please gourmets, the Flamingo prepares prime ribs to achieve maximum tenderness and retain natural juice. They use 18- to 22-pound roasts (smaller one can be used), aged 3 weeks and baked in rock salt. A salt paste is prepared by soaking the rock salt in water for 1 week, then adding flour to make a paste. Roast is placed in a shallow pan, packed with salt paste and roasted at 325° to taste. After removing from the oven, the salt is cut away and the prime ribs are ready to serve. Natural juices are retained and shrinkage is reduced up to 20 per cent by using this process. For juice, take beef trimmings and bones, add cold water and an onion and bring to a boil. Next add seasoning to taste and caramel coloring and let simmer at least 6 hours. Remove from heat and pour over ice cubes to remove all grease. Reheat and pour over each serving.

The Ranch, Devils Lake

Lloyd and Maxine Engh converted an old barn into an interesting restaurant a half-mile south of Devils Lake, a town surrounded by lakes and offering excellent fishing and hunting. Also of tourist interest is Sully's Hill National Wild Life Preserve, a refuge and breeding ground for bison, deer, elk, and wild fowl. The restaurant, located a quarter-mile south of U.S. Highway 2 on State Highway 20, is open for dinner weekdays from 5:30 P.M. to 11:30 P.M. Closed on Sunday and most holidays. Painting by Elsa Hertel.

Ranch Roquefort Dressing
 2 cups sour cream
 2 cups mayonnaise
 ½ pound Roquefort cheese

Combine sour cream and mayonnaise. Crumble cheese into mixture and blend thoroughly. Store in refrigerator.

Garlic Toast

Slice day-old buns or dinner rolls to suit. Brush heavily with melted butter. Sprinkle with garlic salt and toast on heavy metal pan in 400° oven until brown.

Mac's Restaurant, Jamestown

For over thirty years the MacKenzie family has operated a restaurant in Jamestown. Now in a new building on U.S. 281 at I-94 (805 20th Street S.W.), it is an excellent family restaurant stop. Open daily 7:00 A.M. to midnight; Sunday closing at 8:30 P.M. Painting by Harvey Kidder.

Hot German Potato Salad

4 pounds potatoes
3 medium onions, coarsely chopped
$3/4$ cup sugar
salt and black pepper, to taste
$1/2$ pound bacon, diced
$3/4$ cup very hot water
$3/4$ cup cider vinegar
hard-boiled eggs and greens for garnish

Boil potatoes until tender; pare and slice while still warm. Heap chopped onion in center of potatoes. Top with sugar, salt and pepper. Fry diced bacon until crisp. Skim bacon from frying pan and set aside. Add water and vinegar to bacon grease and bring to a boil. Pour over potatoes and onions and toss lightly to mix well. Add bacon and garnish with hard-boiled eggs and greens. Serves 8–10.

Ham and Pineapple Rolls

Flour 8 pineapple spears and brown in 3 tablespoons butter. Then roll each spear in a ham slice and secure with a toothpick. Bake in 350° oven for 30 minutes. Pour 1 cup heavy cream over dish and bake for another 15 minutes, basting once.

San-Dar Smorgasbord, Bellville

Five days a week this restaurant is open and offers a smorgasbord of over 125 dishes, including 35 desserts. In one of Ohio's areas rich in recreation facilities, it is midway between Cleveland and Columbus, a few miles southeast of Interstate 71, on State Highways 13 and 97 in the center of Bellville. Open weekdays 5:00 P.M. to 9:00 P.M.; Sunday noon to 7:00 P.M. Closed Monday and Tuesday; closed from December 20 to middle of March. Painting by Wucius Wong.

Dutch Apple Dessert
8   apples
1   cup brown sugar
$^1/_2$ cup white sugar
1   teaspoon cinnamon
$^1/_2$ teaspoon nutmeg
3   tablespoons flour
1   cup heavy cream

Wash and pare apples and slice into a mixing bowl. Add sugars, cinnamon, nutmeg, flour and cream. Mix well and pour into two 10-inch round baking dishes. Cover with topping.

Topping
Combine 1 cup brown sugar, 3 tablespoons butter and 1 cup flour. Mix ingredients to the consistency of pie dough. Sprinkle over mixture in pan and garnish with $^1/_2$ cup pecan halves. Bake in preheated 375° oven for 10 minutes, then reduce to 350° and bake about 40 minutes, or until apples are tender. Serves 8–10.

Eaton Manor, Hamilton

Lunch and dinner served every day until midnight at this popular and pleasant restaurant at 1892 Dixie Highway (State Highway 4) in Hamilton. A smorgasbord is a featured attraction on Saturday evening and all day Sunday. Closed only on Christmas Day. It is about seven miles west of Interstate Highway 75. Painting by Edwin Fulwider.

Ice Cream Tropicana

Crumb Mixture
- 1   cup graham-cracker crumbs
- 1/4   cup flaked coconut
- 1/4   cup pecans, coarsely chopped
- 1 1/2 tablespoons sugar
- 1/4   teaspoon ground cinnamon
- 1/4   teaspoon ground mace
- 1/4   cup melted butter

Place first 6 ingredients in a bowl. Add melted butter; toss lightly with a fork. Cover and set aside at room temperature.

Fruit Mixture
- 1   cup strawberries, sliced
- 1   cup seeded or seedless grapes, sliced
- 1   cup pineapple chunks
- 1/3   cup sugar
- 1   lemon, juice and grated rind

Place fruits in bowl. Thoroughly blend sugar with lemon rind; add, with juice, to fruits and toss so that fruit is thoroughly coated. Cover and chill.

Divide 1 quart of vanilla ice cream into 6-8 portions. Top each portion with fruit mixture and then sprinkle each with portion of crumb mixture.

Leonello Restaurant, Shaker Heights

Oil reproductions of some of the world's most famous art line the dining room walls of this establishment at 16713 Chagrin Boulevard in Shaker Heights, a suburb of Cleveland. Leonello Giuriati, the owner-manager, welcomes guests at dinner, which is served daily except Sunday from 6:00 P.M. to 10:30 P.M. Reservations necessary. Painting by Peter Dubaniewicz.

**Fillet of Beef en Brochette
with Mushroom Sauce**
2 pounds fillet of beef, cut into
    1-inch cubes
2 onions, cut in pieces
1 green pepper, cut in pieces
30 mushroom caps
Alternate above ingredients on 4 skewers. Broil until cooked to taste.

Serve covered with mushroom sauce prepared as follows:

Mushroom Sauce
Melt $\frac{1}{4}$ pound butter in a skillet, add 1 cup sliced mushrooms and sauté. Season to taste with salt and pepper and continue cooking over low heat. Add 2 tablespoons sherry. Serves 4.

Wooster Inn, Wooster

Overlooking the college golf course, this delightful country-style inn is on the campus of the college of Wooster, in Wooster, Ohio. Opened in the fall of 1959, it offers lodging and dining in a relaxed atmosphere. Open every day except Christmas, for breakfast, lunch and dinner. Dining room closed first two weeks of July. Overnight accommodations and recreation facilities. Reservations recommended for meals and rooms. Painting by Ray Naylor.

Chicken Paprikash

- 4 two-pound oven-ready chickens
- ¹/₂ pound butter
- ¹/₄ cup sliced carrots
- ¹/₄ cup chopped celery
- ¹/₄ cup chopped onions
- 1 cup flour
- 2 teaspoons paprika
- 1 quart chicken broth
- ¹/₂ pint sour cream
- salt, pepper and garlic to taste
- cooked noodles or steamed rice

Cut the chickens in half and brown on both sides in skillet in a little butter. Drain. Place in baking pan and cover with following sauce:

Sauce

In the same skillet, sauté carrots, celery and onions until tender. Melt the remaining butter and cook the flour and paprika until light brown; pour in chicken broth and vegetables and cook until smooth. Then mix in sour cream. Pour the sauce over the chicken and bake in 325° oven for 45 minutes. The chicken is then served on cooked noodles or steamed rice. Serves 8.

Chef Louie's Steak House, Mitchell

For over 40 years, this restaurant in Mitchell has been noted for its good food served in a friendly atmosphere. At 601 East Havens — the intersection of U.S. Highway 16 and State Highway 37 — it is open every weekday for dinner from 4:30 P.M. to 11:00 P.M. Closed on Sunday. Marguerite Russell is the owner and manager. Painting by Bill J. Hammon.

Pheasant with Wild Rice

1/2 pheasant (per serving)
flour, seasoned with salt, pepper, paprika and monosodium glutamate
mixture of 3/4 cup of milk with 1 beaten egg
deep fat
wild rice
parsley for garnish

Cut each half pheasant into 4 serving pieces. Remove skin. (If pheasant is frozen, first partially thaw in hot water.) Dredge in seasoned flour, then dip in egg and milk mixture. Dredge again in flour. Brown in deep fat for 8 minutes, then steam at low pressure in stove-top roaster for 15 minutes. Serve each portion with 3½ ounces wild rice. Garnish with parsley.

The Abbey, Fontana, Lake Geneva

This year-around resort on the shore of Lake Geneva offers guests majestic floor-to-ceiling views of water, beach, and oak-shaded lawns. Open to the public as well as guests are three restaurants and three cocktail lounges. Breakfast, lunch and dinner are served daily. Reservations necessary both for meals and overnight accommodations. Follow road sign to Lake Geneva. Painting by Frederick H. Malloy.

**Chicken Breast Sauté
au Champagne**
4 8-ounce chicken breasts
2 tablespoons butter
1 teaspoon shallot, chopped
2 cups champagne
2 cups demiglaze sauce (brown
  sauce)
1 cup heavy cream
4 pieces of toast
4 slices truffle
4 mushroom caps, sautéed in
  butter
rice pilaf

Season chicken breasts with salt and pepper, then sauté in butter, until slightly brown. Add shallots. Cover with champagne. In a separate pan combine demiglaze and heavy cream. Cook over medium heat until reduced slightly. Pour cream mixture onto chicken and cook until chicken is tender, 15-20 minutes. Serve chicken breasts on toast topped with a slice of truffle, mushroom cap, and champagne sauce. Garnish with pilaf. Serves 4.

Manitowoc Motor Hotel, Manitowoc

Located at 204 N. 8th Street, featuring the Caravan Room as the main dining room. Open from 6:30 A.M. to 9:00 P.M., seven days a week, serving breakfast, lunch and dinner. Lake Michigan and Point Beach State Park are nearby attractions. The closest main highways are U.S. 10 and 151. Painting by C. L. Peterson.

Chocolate Ice Box Torte
Crust

2¹/₂ cups graham-cracker crumbs
¹/₂ cup sifted powdered sugar
1 teaspoon cinnamon
³/₄ cup melted butter

Combine ingredients, and butter a 10-inch torte pan (2¹/₂ inches deep) and line bottom and sides with mixture. Bake 15 minutes at 350°. Cool.

Filling

Dissolve 2 envelopes gelatin in ¹/₂ cup of cold water. Cut 4 squares of bitter chocolate in small pieces, then pour 1 cup boiling water over them. Stir until chocolate is melted, then add gelatin mixture. Beat 8 egg yolks well and add 1 cup sugar. Stir into chocolate mixture. To this add ¹/₂ cup toasted chopped pecans and 2 teaspoons vanilla. Beat 8 egg whites very stiff, slowly adding 1 cup of sugar as whites are beaten. Fold whites into chocolate mixture, pour into crust and chill thoroughly. The recipe makes 20 portions.

Alpine Village, Mequon

The Buchels, four Swiss-American brothers, built their old-country Swiss tavern on a four-acre estate, twelve miles north of Milwaukee on State Highway 57 in Mequon. The brothers piped a fresh spring into the dining-kitchen area to make a pond, and stocked it with brook trout. Guests may catch their own dinner for the cooks to prepare. Dinner served daily; reservations may be made for private luncheon parties. Painting by John Warren.

Swiss Fondue
- 1 pound sharp Cheddar cheese, grated
- 1 pound aged Swiss cheese, grated
- 1 cup white wine
- 1 teaspoon dry mustard
- 1/2 teaspoon garlic, chopped
- dash of Tabasco sauce
- dash of Worcestershire sauce
- toast squares

Combine ingredients in a saucepan and cook over low fire until smooth. Add 1 ounce kirsch and serve immediately on hot toast. Or serve Swiss style — dip pieces of French bread into bubbling fondue in a chafing dish. Serves 12.

Club Riversite, Mequon

The charm of this restaurant lies in the warm personalities of the owners, Mr. and Mrs. Gene Buchel and Chef Walter Buchel. They came as young people from Switzerland and have devoted their lives to the preparation and serving of good food. Only ten miles north of Milwaukee, it is on State Highway 57 (11140 N. Cedarburg Road) in Mequon. Open for dinner only from 5:00 P.M. to 10:30 P.M.; reservations necessary. Closed on Sunday and major holidays. Painting by Doris A. White.

Rich Apple Coffee Cake

Mix together like piecrust: 1¼ cups flour, 1 teaspoon sugar, ½ teaspoon salt, 1 teaspoon baking powder and ¼-pound butter. Add 2 teaspoons milk and 1 egg yolk. Put into ungreased 7″ x 11″ coffeecake pan. Cover with 8 medium baking apples, quartered and laid in rows. Top with mixture of: 1½ tablespoons flour, ¾ cup sugar, 1 teaspoon cinnamon and 2 tablespoons butter. Bake in 375° oven for 45 to 50 minutes.

Beef Tenderloin à la Parisienne

Cut 4 beef tenderloin slices into 1-inch strips. Season with salt and pepper to taste. Sauté in butter to individual preference. Meanwhile sauté in butter in another pan: 2 each, green peppers and tomatoes in ½ inch cubes; 1 cup mushrooms; garlic, to taste. Cook 4-5 minutes, then add 1 cup lightly thickened meat gravy and pour over meat. Serve with potatoes, noodles or rice. Makes 2 portions.

Frenchy's Restaurant, Milwaukee

Paul LaPointe is the owner of this popular restaurant, which serves excellent French and American food, and game in season. Open every day from 11:30 A.M. to 1:00 A.M.; reservations necessary. Closed Christmas Eve and Christmas Day. The address is 1901 East North Avenue, two blocks west of Wisconsin State Highway 32 (N. Prospect Avenue). Painting by C. L. Peterson.

Braised Calves' Sweetbreads in Wine Sauce

2   pounds sweetbreads
chicken stock or water to cover
1   bay leaf
4   peppercorns
2   ounces chopped raw onion
    (not green or dehydrated)
1/2 blade celery, chopped, or
    celery tops
flour
shortening
24 ounces chicken gravy (or
    thickened chicken bouillon)
2   ounces sherry
12 medium-size mushroom caps

Parboil sweetbreads 15 minutes in water or chicken stock with bay leaf, peppercorns, onion and celery. Let cool. Remove from stock, trim, dry, season and flour lightly. Sauté in shortening until golden brown. Drain balance of shortening, add chicken gravy and let simmer for 5 minutes. Add sherry 5 minutes before serving. Mushrooms may be browned in pan with sweetbreads or may be cooked separately and added to sweetbreads and gravy. Serves 4–6.

Karl Ratzsch's Old World Restaurant, Milwaukee

Strauss waltzes, played nightly and on Sunday afternoon by a Viennese string trio, are only part of the Old World gemütlichkeit that has characterized this restaurant since 1904. Luncheon and dinner are served from 11:30 A.M. to midnight every day. At 320 E. Mason Street, a half block west of State 32. Painting by John Warren.

Braised Lamb Shank Gemüse

4 lamb shanks, ³/₄ to 1 pound each
bouquet garni (2 bay leaves, 2
mashed garlic cloves, 1 dozen
peppercorns, ¹/₄ teaspoon summer savory, ¹/₄ teaspoon thyme
and ¹/₄ teaspoon marjoram, in
cheesecloth bag)
1 cup each: diced onion, celery
and carrots
red wine and beef stock, equal
parts
1 cup each: peas and green beans
flour, to thicken
Kitchen Bouquet and salt, to taste

Sauté lamb shanks till well browned, place in Dutch oven with bouquet garni, onions, carrots, celery and enough wine and stock to cover. Braise in oven at 375° covered, until lamb shanks are tender, about 2¹/₂ hours. In the last half-hour of cooking add peas and beans, and remove bouquet garni. Blend in flour-and-water mixture (1 tablespoon flour with ¹/₄ cup water for each cup of liquid, to thicken). Add Kitchen Bouquet to desired brownness, and salt to taste. Serves 4.

Arkansas

Kansas

Louisiana

Mississippi

Missouri

Texas

Contrasts are sharp in this region. Here you will find the highly seasoned dishes that are of Mexican origin, the epicurean creations of the Creoles, the imaginative seafood recipes of the Gulf Coast, and the plain but satisfying fare of the Ozarks and farm country. Menus offer delicacies that range from Oysters à la Popine and Shrimp Creole to Green Enchiladas and Texas Pecan Pie. This is not a region for the light eater.

SOUTH
CENTRAL

Holiday Inn, Harrison

In the heart of the Ozark vacation country, this motor hotel in downtown Harrison is on U.S. Highways 62 and 65 North. Vacationists here are close to such attractions as tours of Ozark Mountain trails, float trips, fishing and numberless scenic caves and waterfalls. The dining room is open daily from 6:00 A.M. to 10:00 P.M., and is noted for its wholesome food with a "good old-fashioned country flavor." Overnight accommodations and vacation facilities. Painting by Paul Brewer.

Fruit Cocktail Cake
4 cups flour
2 cups sugar
2 teaspoons baking soda
1 No. 2½ can fruit cocktail, undrained

Mix ingredients with a spoon, then pour into 9" x 13" greased pan. Before placing in oven cover with topping below.

Topping
Combine: ½ cup light brown sugar, ½ cup coconut and ½ cup chopped pecans. Sprinkle on top of unbaked cake. Bake in 300° oven for 45 minutes, or until cake springs back at touch. While cake is still warm, spread with frosting below.

Frosting
Combine: 1 cup sugar, 1 small can evaporated milk, ½ cup butter and 1 teaspoon vanilla. Cook over medium fire until thick, then spread on warm cake.

Red Rooster Restaurant, Hutchinson

Hearty homemade soups, breads, pastries, and ice cream are a few of the specialties at this attractive restaurant which serves family-style chicken dinners at 1808 North Plum Street. From U.S. Highway 50 take Plum Street north for 14 blocks. Meals served 11:00 A.M. to 8:00 P.M. every day except Monday. Closed on Thanksgiving and Christmas Day. (Carry-out chicken boxes are available for tourists who want to enjoy a picnic.) Painting by Robert Kranz.

Bulgur Pecan Pie
3   eggs
¼ cup vegetable oil
½ cup brown sugar
1   cup maple syrup
¾ cup milk
1   teaspoon vanilla
½ teaspoon salt
¼ cup bulgur
1   cup pecans
9-inch pie shell, unbaked

Beat eggs, then mix in all remaining ingredients in order given. Pour into an unbaked pie shell, and bake at 350° for 35 to 40 minutes.

(Bulgur is an ancient food, resembling cracked wheat, developed for modern taste by the Kansas Wheat Commission. The Red Rooster is developing new recipes using it. It is generally available at specialty stores.)

Restaurant Normandie, Lafayette

Located on the grounds of the Plantation Motor Hotel on U.S. Highway 90 (1211 Pinhook Road) in Lafayette. Real French bread and croissants are just a sample of the gourmet fare enjoyed by guests. G. A. Cabé-Maury is the owner. Open from 11:00 A.M. to 2:00 P.M. and from 6:00 P.M. to 10:30 P.M. Monday, Tuesday and Wednesday during the racetrack season on race nights. Thursday, Friday and Saturday reopens at 5:30 P.M. Open Sunday from 11:00 A.M. to 2:30 P.M. Painting by Ben Earl Looney.

Frog Legs Bercy
Take 2 pairs of frog legs, 5 to 6 inches long, and dry in a towel. Melt a spoonful of butter in a frying pan and bring to a gold color on medium fire. Season with a little salt and pepper and touch of garlic. (Do not use garlic sauce or salt.) Brown the frog legs, turning them often; when brown, place frying pan in a preheated 400° oven for 15 minutes.

Sauce
Take a frying pan and brown a spoonful of butter, then add $2/3$ cup of fresh mushrooms, 6 ounces of white Chablis or any other dry white wine. Stir in salt and pepper and a little fresh garlic. Pour sauce over frog legs and put back in the oven for 4 to 5 minutes.

To serve, take an oval serving dish, place frog legs one on top of another in a line, and pour a small amount of the sauce on top of the frog legs and the remainder of the sauce around them. Sprinkle with chopped parsley and serve. Serves 1.

Bali Ha'i at the Beach, New Orleans

On the midway of Pontchartrain Beach, the South's largest amusement center, this is New Orleans' only authentic South Sea Island eating place. The owner, Harry J. Batt, Sr., selected all of the building's decor while on his extensive trips through the South Seas. The food is prepared by master chefs who offer a complete American menu in addition to the exotic cuisine of the South Pacific. The restaurant is on Lakeshore Drive, a mile north of U.S. 90, overlooking Pontchartrain Beach. Open for dinner from 5:00 P.M. to 11:30 P.M. every day in the summer; closed on Monday, September through April. Painting by Don C. Smith.

Steak Kew
3   pounds top-grade sirloin
1/4 cup butter, melted
1   teaspoon soy sauce
1/2 cup canned oyster sauce
1   teaspoon sugar
1/2 cup water chestnuts, sliced
1/2 cup mushrooms, sliced
1   cup Chinese pea pods
1/2 cup bamboo shoots
1/2 cup cornstarch
1/2 cup sherry

The sirloin is cubed in 1-inch squares with *all* fat removed. In pan combine the beef, butter, soy and oyster sauce, sugar, and salt to taste. Cover and sauté for 2 or 3 minutes, or to your personal beef taste. Remove the beef from the pan, add vegetables to the beef stock, and cook over low flame for 2 minutes, adding cornstarch and sherry. Replace beef and cook 2 more minutes. Serves 6.

Cantonese Barbecued Spareribs
Combine: 2 cups sugar, 1/2 cup salt, 1 teaspoon minced garlic, 1 cup Hoisin sauce and 3 tablespoons brown bean sauce. If desired, add a little red food coloring. Cut 5 large pork ribs in two and marinate in above sauce for 3-4 hours. Cook ribs on rotisserie or hang in Chinese oven, basting with marinade as they cook.

The Inn, Opelousas

The Evangeline Terrace is the restaurant at this fine community-owned motor inn in the heart of the Cajun country. Breakfast, lunch and dinner served until 10:00 P.M. daily; a sumptuous seafood buffet on Friday from 6:00 P.M. to 10:00 P.M., and a regular buffet on Sunday from noon to 9:00 P.M. Reservations are necessary for buffets. Overnight accommodations and recreation facilities at the hotel. It is located at 404 East Landry Street (U.S. Highway 190) in Opelousas. Painting by Don C. Smith.

Oysters à La Popine

- ½ cup vegetable-oil shortening
- ½ cup sifted all-purpose flour
- ½ cup green onions, finely chopped
- ½ cup sweet peppers, finely chopped
- 1 tablespoon garlic, finely chopped
- 3 cups medium oysters
- ¼ teaspoon Tabasco, or equal pepper sauce
- salt to taste
- 3 cups steamed rice

Using low heat in heavy skillet, prepare roux with shortening and flour, using water as necessary to maintain liquid consistency. Slowly add onions, stir constantly for 15 minutes. Add peppers and stir for 10 minutes. Add chopped garlic and stir for 5 minutes. Add oysters and increase heat to permit oysters to cook 5 minutes. Lower heat, add Tabasco and simmer 10 minutes. Season with salt to taste. Serve over hot rice immediately. Serves 4.

Sansone's Restaurant, Shreveport

For over twenty years this restaurant in the center of Shreveport at 701 East Kings Highway (State Highway 3032) has been noted for its fine seafood, steaks, and Continental cuisine. The focal point of the dining room is a fountain of imported Italian glass. Open every day from 11:00 A.M. to midnight. Tony Sansone and Vito Cefalu are owners and managers. Painting by Paul Brewer.

Trout à la Vito
Take 4 medium fillets of sea trout, flour lightly, salt and pepper and sauté until golden brown in butter. Remove from heat. Place 3 ounces of lump crabmeat in a saucepan and add 4 tablespoons of butter, juice of $1/2$ lemon, a pinch of oregano, and salt and white pepper. Add $1^1/_2$ teaspoons of Lea & Perrins Sauce and simmer, taking care not to destroy the texture of the lumps of crabmeat. Add 2 tablespoons of dry sherry and sauté for 2 minutes. Pour this mixture over the trout and sprinkle with sliced almonds and a little minced parsley. Serves 2.

Scampi alla Siciliana
In a kettle put 6 tablespoons olive oil, 4 cloves of garlic, minced, 4 tablespoons parsley, finely minced, and a pinch of pepper and oregano. Heat together for 2 minutes, then add 12 jumbo shrimp with tails, peeled and deveined. Cover pot and steam shrimp over moderate heat until done (about 5 minutes). Serve shrimp on platter with cooking liquid poured over them. Serves 3.

Mary Mahoney's Old French House Restaurant, Biloxi

A combination of good food served in an antebellum atmosphere has made this three-year-old restaurant, managed by Mary Mahoney, a success from the start. Located in the oldest house in Biloxi, which was built in 1737, it is at 138 Magnolia Street a block north of U.S. 90. Open for lunch and dinner weekdays 11:00 A.M. to 11:00 P.M.; closed Sundays and Christmas. Reservations advisable. Painting by Peter Rex Denby.

Chicken Bonne Femme

4 breasts of chicken
flour
salt and pepper to taste
2 ounces butter
1 bell pepper, sliced
1 clove garlic, chopped fine
$1/2$ teaspoon monosodium glutamate
2 ounces julienne ham
1 medium onion, chopped
1 large potato, peeled and sliced
1 $4^1/_2$-ounce can mushrooms, sliced
4 ounces red wine

Dredge chicken in seasoned flour, brown pieces in butter. Place chicken in Dutch oven with bell pepper, garlic, monosodium glutamate, ham and onion. Place potato slices on top of chicken and sprinkle with mushrooms. Cover and cook over low heat for 45 minutes. When potatoes are done, add wine and let stand for 10 minutes before serving. Serves 4.

Shrimp French House

Chop 1 medium onion and 1 stalk of celery and sauté in butter until tender; add 2 pounds cleaned medium-size shrimp, 1 teaspoon salt, 2 tablespoons monosodium glutamate, and cook for 10 minutes; then add $1/2$ pint of sour cream, 2 tablespoons chili sauce and one small can mushrooms. Stir well, then add 2 teaspoons sherry and let simmer 10 minutes. Serve on bed of spinach noodles or toast points. Sprinkle with chives. Serves 4.

La Font Inn, Pascagoula

One mile east of Pascagoula on U.S. Highway 90, this restaurant and motel are open year around. The dining room serves every day from 6:00 A.M. to 10:00 P.M. There are 100 modern motel units, with a junior Olympic swimming pool and a playground for children. Douglas Fontaine is the owner and manager. The mailing address is P.O. Box 1028, Pascagoula. Painting by F. Wenderoth Saunders.

Macaroon Pie
3 egg whites
1 cup sugar
9 soda crackers, crushed fine
1 cup pecans, chopped
2 teaspoons almond extract
1 tablespoon butter
1 cup whipping cream, whipped

Beat egg whites until frothy. Add sugar gradually and continue beating until stiff. Fold in cracker crumbs, pecans and almond extract. Melt butter in 9-inch pie pan. Pour in mixture. Bake in 300° oven for 20 minutes. Chill. Top with whipped cream, just before serving.

Stan Musial and Biggie's, St. Louis

Stan Musial, former Cardinal baseball star, is one of the owners of this popular St. Louis restaurant. Just south of Forest Park, it is off U.S. 40 — take the Oakland Avenue cut-off and go about eight blocks to 5130. Lunch and dinner daily. Reservations not necessary; tables not held during busy periods. Painting by Robert Johnson.

Cherries Jubilee
20 black Bing cherries, pitted
2 teaspoons sugar
lemon ring (cut from ¼ of lemon peel)
orange ring (cut from ¼ of orange peel)
1 cinnamon stick
1 ounce rum
1 ounce brandy
4 scoops vanilla ice cream
Combine cherries with 4 teaspoons of their juice and sugar. Add lemon and orange rings and cinnamon stick and heat until sugar dissolves, stirring gently so as not to break cherries. Add rum and brandy, reserving 1 teaspoon brandy for flaming. Place reserved brandy in long-handled spoon and ignite, then quickly stir cherries and juice until flame is extinguished. Remove cinnamon stick. Sauce is then spooned over the ice cream and served at once. Serves 4.

The Barn, Austin

There are three dining sections at this interesting restaurant located at 8611 Balcones Drive (four miles northwest of the intersection of Interstate 35 and U.S. Highway 183). One of the first-floor dining rooms has a rustic atmosphere with red-checkered tablecloths while the second floor is more formal in atmosphere. The third, called the Silo, is a formal dining room adjacent to the Barn. Dinner only, served daily. Reservations necessary. Closed Christmas Day. Painting by Mark Storm.

Stuffed Crab

1 tablespoon green onion, chopped
1 tablespoon parsley, chopped
1 tablespoon melted butter
1/2 cup breadcrumbs
1/4 cup milk or cream
1 1/2 cups fresh crabmeat
2 tablespoons lemon juice
1 teaspoon onion juice
1 large, or 2 small, eggs
1/4 teaspoon dry mustard
1/2 teaspoon monosodium glutamate
4-5 crab shells

Sauté chopped onion and parsley in melted butter. Add breadcrumbs and milk. Bring to boil and cook until mixture is thick. Add crabmeat and remaining ingredients. Mixture should be stiff. Pack into crab shells and brush tops with additional melted butter. Brown in 375° oven until golden brown, 15-20 minutes. Serves 4.

The Surrey Inn, Caldwell

Fine antiques are the furnishings in the dining rooms of this inn which is located at the intersection of State Highway 21 (El Camino Real) and State Highway 36 in Caldwell. The location is less than 200 miles from Dallas, an easy four hours' drive. Meals are served every day from 5:00 A.M. to 10:00 P.M. Overnight accommodations and recreation facilities in the attached motor hotel. Painting by Joseph Donaldson.

Old-fashioned Custard Ice Cream

2½ cups sugar
6 eggs
6 tablespoons flour
½ gallon milk
½ pint whipping cream
1 tablespoon vanilla
pinch of salt

Sift flour into sugar, add salt and combine until thoroughly blended. Break eggs, one at a time, into the sugar mixture, stirring lightly with fork until blended. Scald milk in a double boiler, add sugar-and-egg mixture, stirring constantly. Continue stirring until the custard forms a thin coating on the spoon. A wooden spoon is better for stirring custard while it is cooking. Set custard aside to cool. When cool, strain into a gallon freezer, add whipping cream and vanilla. Freeze until firm. Remove the dasher, seal tightly and pack down with ice-cream salt and ice, if it is to be served immediately. Otherwise store in plastic containers in freezer. This ice cream is better if eaten within 1 to 2 days after it is made. Makes about 1 gallon.

Mr. Peppé, Dallas

Small and intimate, with only 10 tables, this restaurant is noted for its excellent French and Continental foods and wines. Art shows are frequent here. Open for dinner every day from 6:00 P.M. to 11:00 P.M. except Sunday. Closed mid-July to mid-August. The address is 5617 W. Lovers Lane. Ernest Bertschi is the owner and manager. Painting by Naomi Brotherton.

Braised Romaine Lettuce

2 heads medium-size romaine lettuce
8 slices bacon
$\frac{1}{2}$ cup onions, sliced
$\frac{1}{4}$ cup celery leaves
1 carrot, peeled, cut lengthwise
1 teaspoon salt
$\frac{1}{4}$ teaspoon pepper
1 cup pot roast sauce or roast beef natural juice
1 cup beef broth

Wash romaine well and carefully without cutting. Parboil lettuce, then drain. Place bacon slices, onions, celery leaves and carrot in pan. Top with lettuce. Add remaining ingredients. Cover. Braise in a 350° oven for an hour. Remove. Cut off ends of lettuce and flatten leaves by gliding flat side of knife over them. Fold lettuce and place on plate. Garnish with vegetables and juice. Serves 4.

Crabmeat Peggy

$\frac{1}{2}$ cup blanched almonds, sliced
$\frac{1}{4}$ cup butter, melted
$6\frac{1}{2}$-ounce can Alaska king crabmeat, fins removed and drained
$\frac{1}{4}$ cup remoulade sauce
1 teaspoon Worcestershire sauce
8 melba toast rounds
lemon and parsley

Pan-fry almonds in butter until slightly browned. Mix in crabmeat and heat until hot. Stir in remoulade sauce and Worcestershire sauce. Serve warm on melba toast. Garnish with lemon and parsley.

Gaidos' Restaurant and Motor Hotel, Galveston

Located on Galveston's Beach Boulevard at 39th street overlooking the Gulf of Mexico, this famous seafood spot has been owned and operated by the Gaido family since 1911. Open every day except Monday for lunch and dinner. Gaidos' own motor hotel next door is open year around; reservations suggested. Painting by Sam Waples.

Shrimp Creole

2 pounds fresh shrimp
2 tablespoons lemon juice
2 tablespoons Worcestershire sauce
2 teaspoons salt
3 tablespoons butter
1 medium-size onion, chopped
1/2 green pepper, chopped
1/2 cup celery, chopped
1 clove garlic minced
2 tablespoons flour
1 teaspoon sugar
1/4 teaspoon pepper
2 dashes Tabasco sauce
2 1/4 cups canned or fresh tomatoes
8 ounces tomato sauce

Shell raw shrimp, devein, sprinkle shrimp with lemon, Worcestershire and 1 teaspoon salt. Melt butter in large frying pan, add onion, green pepper, celery and garlic and sauté over low heat about 5 minutes, or until vegetables are tender. Blend flour, 1 teaspoon salt, sugar, pepper and Tabasco into combined tomatoes and tomato sauce. Cook covered over low heat 15-20 minutes or until flavors are well blended. Add seasoned raw shrimp; cover and cook over low heat 3 to 5 minutes, or until shrimp are firm. Serve over 2 cups hot buttered rice. Serves about 8.

Kaphan's, Houston

Peter Tomac is the owner-manager of this popular restaurant at 7900 South Main Street. A number of appetizing crab dishes are featured here — crabs en brochette, Crab Lorenzo and Crab Imperial. The menu also includes steaks, chicken and various seafoods. Open for lunch and dinner from 11:30 A.M. to 11:30 P.M. every day except Wednesday. Painting by Sam Waples.

Crab Imperial
1   green pepper, diced fine
2   pimentoes, diced fine
1   tablespoon English mustard
1   tablespoon salt
1/2 teaspoon white pepper
2   eggs, lightly beaten
1   teaspoon monosodium glutamate
1   cup mayonnaise
3   pounds lump crabmeat

Combine pepper and pimento. Combine remaining ingredients, except crabmeat, with mayonnaise and then blend in pepper and pimento. Add crabmeat and mix lightly. Fill 8 crab shells or 8 small casseroles with the crabmeat mixture. Top with light coating of additional mayonnaise and sprinkle with paprika. Bake in 350° oven for 15 minutes. Serve either hot or cold. Serves 8.

The Sirloin, Lubbock

As the name suggests, this restaurant is noted for its fine beef. All broiling is done over hickory charcoal to create a penetrating heat which seals in juices and creates a subtle seasoning. The pies served here are baked fresh daily in the Sirloin kitchen and share the spotlight with the prime beef. John D. Smith, Jr., is the owner and manager of this restaurant at 1003 Amarillo Road at the junction of U.S. 87 and North Avenue Q. Painting by Clarence E. Kincaid.

Texas Pecan Pie

2 eggs
1/2 cup sugar
1 cup white corn syrup
1 tablespoon butter
1 teaspoon vanilla extract
1 1/2 cups broken pecans
10-inch unbaked pie shell

Beat eggs, then blend in remaining ingredients. Pour mixture into pie shell. Bake 15 minutes in 450° oven, then bake 45 minutes more at 375°.

Red Barn Steak House, Mathis

On State Highway 9, five miles south of Mathis, this restaurant has an attractive rural atmosphere. The food specialties are steaks, seafood, and homemade salad dressings and relishes. Open weekdays for dinner from 4:30 P.M. to 10:30 P.M.; Sunday hours 3:00 P.M. to 9:00 P.M. Closed on Mondays and Christmas Day. Painting by Jim Kelly.

Red Barn Famous Dressing
2 cups mayonnaise
1 avocado, mashed fine
6 green onions, chopped fine
½ small can anchovies, chopped fine
4 tablespoons buttermilk
1 teaspoon Tabasco
1½ tablespoons Worcestershire sauce
1½ tablespoons soy sauce
1½ teaspoons wine vinegar
¼ lemon, juice
¼ teaspoon each: celery seed, dry mustard, oregano, white pepper, monosodium glutamate, salt, garlic powder, and green coloring (optional).

Mix thoroughly and refrigerate. Makes 1 quart dressing. Excellent on all green salads.

New Braunfels Smokehouse, New Braunfels

Years ago this was a neighborhood smokehouse where local ranchers brought their meat to be cured in the long, slow German way. Its fame grew, and finally in response to public demand, the Dunbar family opened a dining room serving its products, a store, a large mail-order business and, of course, a greatly enlarged smokehouse where the centuries-old method is still used. On U.S. Highway 81, a block west of Interstate 35, the dining room and store are open every day from 7:00 A.M. to 8:00 P.M. Painting by Ralph White.

Smoked Ham "Finesse"
Boil 8 ounces egg noodles. Drain. Grind or chop 2 cups leftover New Braunfels smoked ham (or your own favorite brand). Grease 9-inch baking dish. Arrange boiled noodles and ham in three alternate layers. Combine 2 well-beaten eggs with 1½ cups milk and season with salt and pepper. Pour over noodles and ham and dot top with butter. Bake in 350° oven for 45 minutes. Makes 6 portions.

Smokehouse Special Bacon Sandwich
Toast 2 slices bread on one side. Turn and spread with mayonnaise. Place in layers: 3 slices cooked bacon, 2 thin slices onion and 2 slices tomato. Top with slice of Cheddar cheese and bits of Jalapeño pepper (a hot pepper).

Casa Rio Mexican Foods, San Antonio

Colorful decorations from Mexico form the backdrop for excellent south-of-the-border fare at this delightful restaurant located at 100 W. Commerce Street in downtown San Antonio, two blocks south of U.S. Highway 90. The outdoor patio is on the banks of the San Antonio River, and guests may watch the passing river traffic as they enjoy tacos, tamales, enchiladas and other favorites. Open for lunch and dinner every weekday; closed on Sunday. A. F. Beyer and Johnson Smith are the owners. Painting by Warren Hunter.

Green Enchiladas

Simmer a frying chicken in water seasoned with onion, celery, pepper and salt, to taste. Reserve broth. When done, dice chicken and salt to taste. Grate 1½ pounds Monterey Jack cheese in another container.

Make a sauce by combining the following: 5 pounds tomato fresadilla (a tiny green tomato with dry husk found in Mexican specialty stores); 2 bell peppers, chopped; 3 onions, chopped; 3 chicken-bouillon cubes and 1 pint broth from chicken. Simmer 1 hour and strain. Take 32 tortillas (a Mexican corn pancake) and dip in hot oil. Then put a small portion of chicken and cheese on each tortilla before rolling up. Immediately before serving, heat sauce until it thickens. Pour sauce over enchiladas and top dish with 1 pint of sour cream. Heat for 20 minutes in 400° oven. Serve immediately. Serves 8.

Arizona

California

Colorado

Hawaii

Idaho

Montana

Nevada

New Mexico

Oregon

Utah

Washington

British Columbia

Wyoming

When the pioneers traveled westward they found a land with great natural resources and a lavishly stocked larder. These pioneers were of many nationalities, and they applied their native styles of cookery to the infinite variety of foods they harvested from the fields and orchards, from the sea and the lakes. In this area one finds the best cooking of a dozen nations and unique versions of food favorites transplanted from the older states.

Painting by Edward Reep

WEST

Bright Angel Lodge, Grand Canyon Village

In Grand Canyon National Park, this lodge is on the south rim at Grand Canyon Village on State Highway 64. A comfortable lodge with family units and connecting rooms, it is open all year. Dining room is open for breakfast, lunch and dinner every day; overnight accommodations and excellent vacation facilities. Reservations advisable during the summer months. Painting by Richard Wagner.

Tenderloin Steak Diablo en Brochette

Cut 1½ pounds of beef tenderloin in 1¼-inch cubes. Marinate for 3 hours in following marinade: 2 cups olive oil; 1 cup white wine; 2 bay leaves; 4 whole cloves; 1 clove garlic; 1 medium onion, chopped, and 1 stalk celery. Then place on 4 large skewers in following order — 1 each, mushroom, small onion (cooked or raw), tenderloin cube, pineapple chunk, tenderloin cube, tomato green-pepper square, tenderloin cube, onion and mushroom. Broil 5-10 minutes to suit taste—rare, medium or well done. Serve with Diablo Sauce. Serves 4.

Diablo Sauce

Sauté ¼ dry onion, chopped, 1 stalk celery, chopped, 1 clove garlic, chopped, 2 whole cloves and 1 bay leaf, in 1 ounce of butter for 5 minutes. Add: 1 No. 2 can tomato puree, 1 No. 2 can tomato paste and 2 tablespoons Cayenne pepper or Tabasco sauce. Boil for 10 minutes and strain.

Saddleback Inn, Phoenix

The decorations and furnishings of this new restaurant are reminiscent of the early territorial days of Arizona. The menu features Spanish and Mexican dishes. In the Biltmore Shopping Center, the address is 2420 East Camelback. It is open until 11:00 P.M. every day, serving breakfast, lunch and dinner. Painting by Rex Brandt.

Chicken Veracruz
Bone ten 8-ounce chicken breasts. Pound with a wooden mallet until chicken is about 1/2 inch thick. Marinate for 24 hours in the following mixture: 1 quart oil; 1 cup sherry; 2 cloves garlic; 1 tablespoon black pepper; pinch of salt and a dash of paprika and oregano. Sauté marinated chicken in butter until brown on both sides. Bake uncovered in 350° oven for 10 minutes. Serve with broiled tomatoes, sliced avocado, rum-fried bananas, and Rice Ortega (recipe follows). Serves 10.

Rice Ortega
Sauté 1/2 cup chopped onions until light brown in 3 tablespoons butter. Add 4 cups cooked rice; 1 small Jalapeño pepper, finely ground (or other small hot red or green pepper); 1 3/4 cups sour cream; 1/2 pound cottage cheese; 1/2 pound grated longhorn cheese; 1/2 bay leaf, crumbled; salt and pepper. Alternate layers of rice mixture and canned Ortega chili strips to form 4 layers in greased casserole. Bake at 375° for 25 minutes. Top with 1/2 cup additional grated cheese and bake for 10 minutes. Makes 10 portions.

Coat of Arms, Tucson

It is easy to forget the heat of the nearby desert when strolling through the Florentine architecture of Casas Adobes Plaza, the setting for this restaurant located at 7053 North Oracle Road. It is seven miles north of the heart of the city on U.S. 89. Open every day for lunch and dinner, 11:00 A.M. to 1:00 A.M., including Sunday. Painting by Davis Sorokin.

Sliced Beef Tenderloin à la Jon

1 medium bell pepper, shredded
1/2 medium onion, shredded
4 ounces fresh mushrooms, sliced
2 cloves garlic, chopped fine
2 tablespoons butter
1 pound beef tenderloin, sliced
  1/8 inch thick
salt and pepper
flour
2 ounces Burgundy
4 ounces beef broth

Slowly sauté pepper, onion, mushrooms and garlic in 1 tablespoon butter. Season tenderloin slices and dust with flour. In another pan sauté meat in 1 tablespoon butter very quickly in very hot pan. Add contents of first pan, then Burgundy and beef broth. Heat over low fire and serve. Serves 4.

The Old Adobe Patio Restaurant, Tucson

When the weather is warm, diners eat outside on the patio under fig trees. Mexican specialties are featured. Open daily except Sunday for luncheon, tea and dinner January through May. Open weekdays only for luncheon June and July; closed all of August and on national holidays. Open daily except Sunday for luncheon September through December. The address is 40 West Broadway in the heart of downtown Tucson, just a half block west of U.S. Highways 80 and 89. Painting by Davis Sorokin.

Almendrado (a Mexican dessert)

2 envelopes gelatin
1 cup cold water
9 egg whites, room temperature
1³/₄ cups sugar
pinch of salt
3 drops almond extract
red and green vegetable coloring
¹/₄ pound blanched almonds, ground

Soak gelatin in cold water. Set over hot water to liquefy and then cool, stirring occasionally until it reaches the consistency of syrup (if too hot, gelatin will thin egg whites too much). Whip egg whites until stiff. Add sugar, salt, gelatin and flavoring, folding into the egg whites. Divide into three bowls. Color one part red or pink, one green, and to the remaining white mixture add ground almonds. Pour in alternately colored layers into a loaf-shaped dish, making the center layer white. Chill in refrigerator, and when firmly set, slice like brick ice cream and top with almond-flavored Custard Sauce, below. Makes 18 servings — try it for your next party.

Custard Sauce for Almendrado

6 egg yolks
¹/₄ cup sugar
¹/₈ teaspoon salt
2 cups scalded milk
¹/₄ teaspoon almond flavoring

Beat egg yolks slightly with a silver fork; add sugar and salt. Add milk gradually, stirring constantly. Cook and stir in double boiler over hot, but not boiling, water until mixture coats the spoon, about 7 minutes. Add the flavoring and chill.

Bar 7 Rancho, Wickenburg

An impressive array of Indian artifacts is on display in the Kachina Room of this establishment, which is on combined U.S. Highway 60, 70, 89 and 93 (111-113 E. Center Street). Lunch and dinner served every day except Tuesday. The bar is open every day. A. W. Prince and Peggy Bratton are the owner-managers. Painting by Robert Atwood.

Biftek à la Mexicana

1½ pounds top sirloin steak
     (½ inch thick)
½ cup flour
1 teaspoon salt
¼ teaspoon pepper
1 clove garlic, minced
1 large onion, sliced thin
½ green pepper, sliced thin
⅓ cup shortening
2 cups canned tomatoes
6 pickled chili peppers
⅓ cup stuffed green olives

Trim fat from meat. Combine flour, salt and pepper. Pound half of seasoned flour into one side of meat, then turn over and pound flour into the other side. Cut meat into servings. Into heavy skillet place garlic, onion, green pepper and shortening and cook until vegetables are wilted. Remove vegetables and in remaining fat brown meat quickly to a deep brown on both sides. Lower heat. Add cooked garlic, onion and green pepper, remaining seasoned flour and canned tomatoes. Cover and cook slowly until meat is tender, about 1½ hours. Add pickled chili peppers and stuffed green olives. If sauce is too thick it can be thinned with tomatoes. Serves 6.

Rancho de los Caballeros, Wickenburg

This 21,000-acre complex combines all of the luxury of the finest resort with the atmosphere and hospitality of a working ranch. Go two miles north of Wickenburg on U.S. Highways 60-70, and then two miles west on the Vulture Mine Road. Open for breakfast, lunch and dinner. Overnight accommodations and vacation facilities. Open from October 15 through April. Reservations necessary for meals and rooms. Painting by Roy Head.

Nut Torte

Beat 4 egg yolks until thick, adding 1 cup sugar and beating until very thick. Add: 1 tablespoon orange juice, 2 tablespoons flour, 1/4 teaspoon salt, 1/2 teaspoon baking powder and 2 cups ground pecans (measure after grinding). Fold in 4 stiffly beaten egg whites. Bake 20-25 minutes in two 9-inch cake pans in a 350° oven. Pans must be greased, lined with paper and greased again. Carefully turn out, and remove paper while torte is warm.

Filling

Combine 1/2 cup whipping cream, whipped, with 1 1/2 teaspoons grated orange rind. Spread between cooled layers.

Frosting

Melt 1 cup chocolate chips over hot water. Stir in 1/2 cup of dairy sour cream. Use to frost top and sides of torte. Torte serves 10-14 and is very rich.

West

Knott's Berry Farm, Buena Park

This famous resort on State Highway 39, easily reached from Los Angeles by three freeways, has grown from a roadside fruit and preserve stand into a tourist attraction rivaling nearby Disneyland. A reconstructed Western .ghost town includes numerous shops, a narrow-gauge railroad, even a working gold mine. Open every day except Christmas for all meals; dinner served noon to 8:30 P.M. Painting by Art Riley.

Mrs. Knott's Old-Fashioned Pioneer Beef Stew

2   pounds stew meat, cubed
1   cup flour
6   cups fresh carrot, diced
2   cups fresh onion, diced
1   No. 2 can green lima beans
1   No. 2$^1/_2$ can tomatoes
$^3/_4$ teaspoon white pepper
$^1/_2$ teaspoon garlic powder
1   teaspoon monosodium glutamate
1   teaspoon celery salt
1   tablespoon salt

Roll meat in flour and steam in pressure cooker (with vent open) for 2 hours. In a separate container cook fresh vegetables together until tender.

Add lima beans and tomatoes to steamed meat. Combine all cooked ingredients. Add seasonings and simmer a few minutes. (If a pressure cooker is not used, brown meat in hot oil and then simmer all ingredients together until beef is tender.) Serves 8.

Cherry Rhubarb Sauce

Wash, do not peel, 1 pound cherry rhubarb; add 2$^1/_4$ cups water and 1$^1/_2$ cups sugar. Cook in open kettle 1-2 minutes after it boils; time will depend on condition of rhubarb. If lid is put on kettle, rhubarb will mash. Let stand a few hours before serving, so that rhubarb will absorb sugar from the juice.

Timber Cove Inn, near Fort Ross

Surrounded by 800 acres of rocky cliffs and wooded plateaus, this handsome inn overlooks the Pacific Ocean. It is open daily for lunch and dinner except from December 15 to April 1. Its location is 82 miles north of San Francisco and three miles north of Fort Ross on State Highway 1. Accommodations are available. Chuck Lyons is the owner. Painting by Dick Moore.

Abalone Giovanni

Warm 8 ounces king crabmeat in 1 cup sweet butter in saucepan. In another pan, warm 1/2 cup sauterne with 1/2 cup each of pineapple and peach juice. Add 2 fresh tomatoes, peeled and cut into 8 wedges each; 4 pineapple slices, cut but not diced; and 3 peaches (fresh or canned), sliced. Mix 1 tablespoon cornstarch with a little water and thicken sauce. (Add red food coloring if more color is desired.) Pound 8 small abalone slices, *on one side only*. Combine pinch each of salt, pepper, onion powder and garlic powder with 1 cup flour in a flat dish. Beat 2 eggs, then dip abalone slices in flour, egg, and flour again. Fry slices in 1 cup sweet oil long enough to brown both sides, about 15 seconds on each side. For each serving, top slice of abalone with 2 ounces warmed crab and a second abalone slice. Ladle or pour equal portions of sauce mixture over each portion. Serves 4.

Imperial Dynasty and Chinese Pagoda, Hanford

One of the last restaurants of the old pioneer era, this eating place in downtown Hanford first opened in 1883. The third generation of the Wing family — Ernest, Harriet, and Richard — are the present owners. The Imperial Dynasty dining room features only Chinese food, and the Chinese Pagoda serves Continental cuisine. The address is 2 China Alley in Hanford's Chinatown. Open for lunch and dinner daily, except Monday. Closed Christmas Day and Chinese New Year. Painting by Brooks Bloomer.

Escargots

(This recipe won the Cordon Bleu Award from the Wine and Food Society of Southern California.)

- 1 pound butter, melted
- 2 tablespoons parsley, minced
- 6-8 pieces fresh garlic, minced
- 1/3 teaspoon nutmeg
- 1 can (72) escargots (French snails and shells)
- 1 tablespoon Dijon mustard
- 1 tablespoon cashew spread
- 1/2 cup cracker meal
- 1 teaspoon dill seed

thin onion slices, chopped and moistened with Chablis

Combine melted butter with parsley, garlic and nutmeg. Pour this marinade over snails and place in cool place overnight. Then stuff snail meat into shells and place on flat broiler pan. Sprinkle each with 1/4 teaspoon cracker meal and a few dill seeds. Top with onion. Put under broiler until piping hot and serve hot with French bread. Serves 12.

The Victor Hugo Inn, Laguna Beach

Situated on a bluff overlooking the shores of Laguna Bay at 361 Cliff Drive, this beautiful restaurant has a setting of three elegant formal gardens. Nearby tourist attractions include Disneyland and Knott's Berry Farm. Open from noon until 9:00 P.M. every day; during July and August open until 10:30 P.M. Reservations advisable in summer. Painting by Art Riley.

Vichyssoise

2½ tablespoons butter
1 small onion, chopped
2 leeks (as white as possible), chopped
1 pint chicken broth
1¼ tablespoons flour
2 potatoes, chopped
salt and pepper to taste
½ cup heavy (40%) cream
1 cup half-and-half
¼ cup chives, chopped

In a soup kettle melt 1 tablespoon butter and sauté onions and leeks without browning them. Add 1 pint chicken broth and bring to a boil. Melt remaining butter and blend in flour to a paste, slowly blend into broth, stirring until smooth. Add potatoes, salt and pepper and cook until potatoes are very soft. Strain soup through a fine sieve and cool immediately. Before serving, mix in cream and half and half. Serve well chilled or hot, as desired, sprinkled with chopped chives. Serves 6.

O'Quinn's of La Mesa, La Mesa

Dining is the main activity here — not even smoking is allowed to spoil the excellent food which has made the O'Quinn's restaurant so popular. Stereo music is selected to entertain rather than for background sound. Lunch and dinner served every day except Tuesday. Reservations advisable Friday and Saturday evenings. The address is 7990 La Mesa Boulevard in the city of La Mesa, a suburb of San Diego. Painting by O. K. Harry.

Roast Beef (or Lamb) Croquettes with Creole Sauce

2 pounds roast beef (or lamb)
2 medium-size onions
3 whole eggs
1/4 cup flour
 breadcrumbs, toasted

Trim all fat and gristle from roast. Grind meat and onion together on medium. Blend in eggs and flour. Shape into croquettes and roll in toasted breadcrumbs. Fry in deep fat at 350° until brown. Serves 8.

Creole Sauce

Combine 2 cups water, 2 cups tomato puree, 1/2 cup sugar, 1/2 cup vinegar, 1 1/2 cups chopped celery, 1/2 cup chopped onion, 1 1/2 teaspoons salt, 1/4 teaspoon oregano and dash of pepper. Pour into saucepan and bring to rolling boil. Turn down to simmer for about 2 hours. A few minutes before serving, thicken with 6 tablespoons cornstarch dissolved in 1 cup of water. Ladle over croquettes.

O'Quinn's Dining Room

Center Club, Los Angeles

On the sixteenth floor of the Kirkeby Center in Los Angeles, this beautiful restaurant offers an extraordinary panorama of the city. It is just east of the San Diego Freeway at the corner of Wilshire and Westwood boulevards at 10889 Wilshire. Open every weekday for lunch from noon to 3:00 P.M.; closed for Sunday lunch. Dinner is served every day from 6:00 P.M. to 11:00 P.M. Reservations advisable. Painting by Jake Lee.

Tournedos Cordon Rouge
Split 6 eight-ounce fillets of beef, horizontally. Wrap each half in a strip of bacon. Season lightly with salt and pepper. Sauté in butter to desired degree—rare, 3 minutes; medium, 5; well, 6. Prepare rounds of bread the same size as tournedos. Toast on both sides in butter. Place slice of ham on each piece of toast, top with beef, a half dollar size slice of foie gras, and Sauce Marchand de Vin. Serve with broiled tomatoes and fresh green beans. Makes 6 portions.

Sauce Marchand de Vin
Sauté $1/3$ cup finely chopped shallots in 4 tablespoons butter until brown. Add $3/4$ cup dry red wine and cook until reduced by half. Add $1 1/2$ cups brown sauce and cook over high heat 8-10 minutes, stirring occasionally. Strain through a sieve and bring to a boil. Turn off heat and stir in 2 tablespoons cold butter to thicken. Yields about 2 cups of sauce.

Granada Grill, Los Angeles

This is the main dining room of the magnificent new Century Plaza Hotel on the Avenue of the Stars, Century City, Los Angeles. The decor is Castilian and the menu features Spanish and American dishes. Breakfast, lunch and dinner served daily from 6:30 A.M. to 11:00 P.M. Reservations necessary. Painting by Noel Tucker.

Paella "Good Friend"

- 1/2 cup olive oil
- 1 4-pound roasting chicken
- salt and pepper to taste
- 6 small onions, chopped
- 1/2 garlic clove, crushed
- 2 1/2 cups raw rice
- 1 bouquet garni
- 1 cup dry white wine
- 5 cups chicken broth
- generous pinch of saffron
- 1 teaspoon oregano
- 4 ounces blanched slivered almonds
- 3/4 cup stuffed olives, chopped
- 12 medium mushrooms, sautéed in 2 ounces butter
- 2 tablespoons chives, chopped

Heat oil. Cut chicken into serving pieces and season with salt and pepper. Sauté until browned. Add onions, garlic and raw rice. Mix well and add bouquet garni. Add white wine, most of chicken broth, saffron and simmer 45 minutes. Sprinkle with oregano, blanched almonds and chopped olives. Add remaining stock, if too dry, remove bouquet garni and sprinkle with mushrooms and chives. Serves 6.

The Stuft Shirt Restaurant, Newport Beach

Located at 2241 W. Coast Highway (U.S. 101), this unusual restaurant is built over the harbor in modern Venetian style, with domes and arches. The view of Balboa Bay is spectacular. Lunch and dinner are served daily. Dock facilities included. Reservations suggested. Painting by James Warren.

Breast of Chicken à la Kiev

Select 3 whole chicken breasts from $3^1/_2$-4-pound roasting chickens; skin, bone and halve them, leaving main wing bone attached. Then place chicken breasts between pieces of waxed paper and pound with a mallet until thin, being careful not to split the flesh. Sprinkle the inside of each with salt, monosodium glutamate and white pepper. Combine 1 tablespoon minced shallots and 1 tablespoon chopped chives. Cut $^1/_4$ pound chilled butter lengthwise into 6 sticks. Place 1 teaspoon of shallot-chive mixture and one portion of butter in the center of each chicken breast. Fold sides and ends in, sealing the butter and allowing the wing bone to protrude. Dredge each portion lightly with seasoned flour, dip into 2 slightly beaten eggs, and coat with breadcrumbs. Using a medium-fry flame, heat $1^1/_2$ cups clarified butter with 1 tablespoon oil and brown chicken breasts quickly on all sides; then place in 400° preheated oven and bake for 10 minutes or until chicken is tender. Drain on absorbent paper. Pour 3 cups Sauce Smitaine (sour cream combined with cream sauce and onions) onto heated serving platter; arrange chicken breasts in sauce and serve immediately. Serves 6.

Del Monte Lodge, Pebble Beach

Separated from Carmel Bay by the eighteenth green of the famous Pebble Beach Golf Links, this luxury resort offers guests six golf courses, swimming, trap and skeet shooting and horseback riding. Hunting and fishing are available in the nearby Santa Lucia Mountains. The dining room is open to the public and serves breakfast, lunch and dinner; reservations advisable. The Lodge is on the Seventeen Mile Drive, which circles the Monterey Peninsula in Northern California. Painting by Link Malmquist.

Del Monte Lodge Lemon Soufflé

2 lemons, rind and juice
1/2 pound white breadcrumbs
1 pint milk
5 ounces sugar
2 ounces butter
4 eggs, separated

Grate lemon rinds on breadcrumbs. Bring milk and sugar to a boil, add breadcrumbs and butter. Let cool. Add juice of lemons and egg yolks. Beat egg whites until firm and fold into mixture. Fill buttered 1 1/2-quart mold 3/4 full. Dust with powdered sugar. Bake in moderate 350° oven for about 1 hour and serve at once. Serves 8.

Doc Clearie's Hilltop Sky Room, Redding

In the Shasta-Cascade recreation area, which boasts year-round fishing, this noted eating place is just ten miles from Shasta Dam and Lake, at the junction of U.S. 99N and State Highway 299E in Redding. Dinner served daily 5:00 P.M. to 11:30 P.M. Address is 10 Hilltop Drive. Painting by Richard Wagner.

Sweetbreads Sautéed with Mushrooms

Drop 1 pound of select sweetbreads into cold water and let stand for 30 minutes. Drain and parboil in 7 parts water and 1 part vinegar with 1 tablespoon chives or onion, until sweetbreads are firm. Drain, then plunge sweetbreads into cold water, removing little strings and membranes. Sauté sweetbreads in about 2 ounces of butter until slightly brown. Add 2 medium green onions, chopped, and 2 ounces sliced mushrooms. Cook 3 minutes more. Add 2 ounces white wine; 4 ounces natural juice of prime rib (or beef broth) and 1 tablespoon of tomato sauce. Cook 10 minutes more and serve at once. Serves 2.

Grenadine of Beef

Coat two 4-ounce half-inch thick fillet steaks with flour. Sauté in light skillet in 1 teaspoon of butter or oil, 3 minutes on each side. Add 2 large button mushrooms and a pinch of salt. Sauté 2 minutes longer. Add 1 teaspoon red wine and 3 tablespoons natural beef juice (or broth). Simmer until sauce is slightly thickened. Serves 1.

Alexis Restaurant, San Francisco

Alexis Merab owns this restaurant, one of San Francisco's finest, which features superb French food served amidst a decor of ancient Byzantine splendor. Entertainment is offered in the Gypsy Cellar. Open from 5:00 P.M. to 2:00 A.M. every weekday; closed on Sunday. It is on Nob Hill at 1001 California Street. Painting by Parker Edwards.

Pheasant Souvaroff
2 2-pound pheasants
pork fat, sliced
salt and pepper to taste
8 ounces imported foie gras, diced
8 medium-size truffles
2 ounces Madeira
1 ounce cognac
1 cup brown chicken gravy
1 pound flour and 1½ cups water, for dough
1 egg yolk

Truss the birds and wrap them in slices of pork fat. Sprinkle with salt and pepper. Roast in 400° oven for 30 minutes. Unwrap birds and stuff them with foie gras. Remove birds to casserole adding truffles previously boiled in Madeira. Drain fat from the pan in which pheasants were roasted. Flambé the stock with cognac, add gravy and Madeira in which truffes were cooked. Pour the sauce over the birds in casserole. Place lid on casserole, seal edges with dough. Brush dough with egg yolk. Place in oven and heat for 15 minutes. Serves 4.

Ernie's Restaurant, San Francisco

All of the mahogany and crystal chandelier splendor of San Francisco's Gilded Age is captured in this fine restaurant owned by Victor and Roland Gotti. Ernie's is open from 6:00 P.M. to midnight seven days a week. The menu features French and Italian cuisine prepared by Chef Paul Quiaud. Located at 847 Montgomery Street. Reservations required. Painting by Alan Atkins.

Chicken Cynthia à la Champagne

2   2½-pound chickens
1   cup flour
1   teaspoon salt
1   tablespoon butter
1   tablespoon oil
1   ounce Curaçao (or other orange-flavored liqueur)
6   ounces dry champagne
1   cup consommé or bouillon
1   cup mushrooms, sliced and sautéed
½   cup whipping cream
orange wedges and seedless grapes, for garnish

Disjoint the chickens. Set wings and legs aside and bone remaining parts. Salt and flour chicken legs and wings and boned parts. Sauté in butter and oil, 10 minutes on each side. Remove from frying pan and continue browning in 350° oven for 20 minutes. Remove from oven and pour on Curaçao and champagne. Then cover with consommé and let chicken simmer on top of stove until tender, about 20 minutes. Add sautéed mushrooms and cream. Garnish with orange wedges and grapes. Serves 4.

The Mandarin, San Francisco

Unlike most Chinese restaurants in America which are Cantonese, the Mandarin features the cuisine of northern China, known as Pekinese or Mandarin. Located at 2209 Polk Street, it is open Tuesday through Friday 5:00 P.M. to 11:00 P.M.; Saturday and Sunday hours are 11:30 A.M. to 11:00 P.M. Reservations required on weekends and for groups of four or more. Some especially complicated dishes must be ordered a day ahead. The owner is Mrs. Sun Yun Chiang. Painting by Link Malmquist.

Beggar's Chicken

Wash a 3-pound chicken. Mix: 2 teaspoons sesame oil, 1 teaspoon cornstarch, 1/4 teaspoon anise seed, and 1/2 teaspoon salt. Rub this mixture over chicken, inside and out. Heat 1 tablespoon sesame oil in a skillet and sauté 1/3 cup dried mushrooms which have been soaked in water 2 hours, then sliced thin. Stir for 2 minutes before adding 1/2 cup boneless pork and 1/4 cup bamboo shoots, both sliced thin. Blend in 1 tablespoon soy sauce and cook for 2 minutes. Stuff this mixture into chicken. Wrap bird in 2 layers of foil and 1 layer of butcher's paper. Encase wrapped chicken in wet clay about 1/4 inch thick. (Ceramic clay may be found at most art supply shops.) Bake in preheated 400° oven for 50 minutes. Lower heat to 200° and bake another hour. To serve, crack clay with mallet and open paper. Serves 4.

Nikko Sukiyaki Restaurant, San Francisco

A few steps from the busy corner of Van Ness and Pine Streets, and you are suddenly in this serene and beautiful Japanese garden restaurant. Lovely kimono-clad girls prepare authentic Japanese dishes in the three dining rooms. Open daily for dinner from 4:00 P.M. to 11:00 P.M. Reservations recommended. Painting by Robert Collins.

Beef Sukiyaki

1 1/2 pound rib steak or top sirloin steak
1 cake tofu (soybean curd), cut in small pieces
1 No. 2 can bamboo shoots, sliced thin
1/2 pound mushrooms, sliced thin
1 pound fresh bean sprouts
1 pound white onions, sliced thin
1 1/2 pounds spinach, cut 2 inches long
2 bunches green onions, 2-inch pieces
(celery and other leaf vegetables may be added if some vegetable items are not available)
1/2 teaspoon monosodium glutamate

Heat a thick 10-inch skillet and melt a piece of beef fat in it. Spread extra-thin beef slices over bottom of pan and sear. After meat is browned add vegetables and other ingredients on top of it. Lower heat. Then add about half of the Sukiyaki Sauce and cook. Let mixture simmer uncovered until the vegetables are cooked. Serve while the vegetables are still crisp. Add remaining Sukiyaki Sauce, a little sugar, sake (rice wine) or sherry to suit your taste. Do not overcook! In Japanese cooking this is important. Serve directly from the pan to the plate. Serves 4.

Sukiyaki Sauce

1/2 cup Japanese soy sauce
1/2 cup consommé or beef stock
2 teaspoons sugar, or to taste
2 ounces sake (Japanese rice wine), or sherry or sauterne

Blend and stir over medium flame until sugar dissolves. Cooking time 6-10 minutes.

Schroeder's Cafe, San Francisco

Established in 1893, Schroeder's restaurant at 240 Front Street maintains a tradition of hearty German food, served in an appropriate setting, with beer steins and mounted stags decorating the walls, and the day's menu written in chalk on blackboards. Max Kniesche is the proprietor. Open Monday through Friday for lunch and dinner, closed on weekends. Men only for lunch; ladies invited after 1:30 P.M. Painting by Parker Edwards.

Roulade of Beef

1   onion
salt and pepper
4   round steaks, $1/2$ pound each and $3/8$ inch thick
$1/4$ teaspoon rosemary
$1/2$ dill pickle
2   ounces salt pork
2   tablespoons shortening
$1/3$ cup flour
2   tablespoons paprika
1   clove garlic
$1/4$ teaspoon thyme
$1/4$ teaspoon marjoram
2   cups beef broth
1   cup tomato puree
1   cup red wine

Dice onion. Salt and pepper the steaks. Add rosemary, and sprinkle half of the diced onion on steaks, along with the half dill pickle, cut in 4 long slices, and salt pork, also cut in 4 slices. Roll steaks, using toothpicks to hold them together. Heat 2 tablespoons of shortening in skillet and brown steaks on both sides. Remove steaks and place in casserole. Fry remaining half of diced onion in skillet, then add flour, paprika, finely chopped garlic clove, thyme, and marjoram, stirring together well. Add beef broth slowly, stirring mixture while pouring, add tomato puree and bring it to a boil. Pour this sauce over steaks in casserole, cover, and bake in 350° oven for two hours. Ten minutes before dish is done, add red wine. Serves 4.

Señor Pico's, San Francisco

Foods of Mexico and early California are featured at this colorful restaurant at 900 North Point, overlooking the new Ghiradelli Square Project and San Francisco Bay. Rodrigo Llorens is the manager. Lunch and dinner served daily; closed on Christmas and Thanksgiving. Painting by Harvey Pell.

Green Enchiladas
Filling

1   pound small-curd cottage cheese
1   pound shredded New York white Cheddar cheese
1   tablespoon chopped cooked onion
1   tablespoon chopped Jalepeña chile
1   tablespoon chopped black olives
$1/2$ teaspoon salt
$1/2$ teaspoon monosodium glutamate

Mix all ingredients thoroughly and set aside.

Sauce

1   No. $2^1/2$ can Ortega chili peppers
1   clove garlic
1   medium-size white onion, cut up
3   quarts chicken stock

2   tablespoons salt
2   tablespoons monosodium glutamate
$1^1/2$ cup flour mixed with 2 cups cold water
1   cup pureed spinach

Puree Ortega chili, garlic and onion in blender. Add this to boiling stock. Thicken with flour-and-water mixture. Add salt, monosodium glutamate and pureed spinach.

Method of Filling and Folding Enchilada:

Dip each of 12 tortillas in hot oil for 1 second to make it soft and keep it from breaking. Place desired amount of filling in center of each tortilla. Roll or fold edges as desired. Place enchilada on baking dish or individual plate. Cover with sauce and put in 375°–400° oven for 10 minutes. Top each enchilada with a tablespoon of sour cream when served. Serves 12.

The Shadows, San Francisco

High on San Francisco's Telegraph Hill, from which diners can see the Bay and the Golden Gate Bridge, this fascinating restaurant occupies a building converted from a sail loft. Dinner served daily 5:00 P.M. to 10:30 P.M. Reservations not accepted. The address is 1349 Montgomery Street. The recipe below is the first one made public in 33 years! Painting by Robert Collins.

Sauerbraten

4 pounds sirloin butt
2 tablespoons salt
1 carrot, peeled and sliced
1 onion, sliced
2 stalks celery, sliced
1 cup red wine vinegar
4 cups water
2 tablespoons pickle spices
1 No. 2 can tomato puree
2 tablespoons paprika
$^{1}/_{2}$ cup currants

Sprinkle salt on meat and brown quickly either in oven or in skillet. Mix remaining ingredients (except puree and paprika) in a bowl, and when meat has cooled, add it to mixture. Marinate for 4 days in refrigerator. Transfer entire mix into cooking pot, add puree and paprika, and simmer slowly until meat is tender. Strain off juices and thicken for gravy, adding currants. Serve meat sliced thick, with gravy. Serve with potato pancakes. Serves 6.

El Poche Cafe, San Gabriel

Down the street from the old San Gabriel Mission and the Mission Play Theatre, this restaurant captures the color and carefree spirit of Mexico. Food is prepared according to techniques brought to California from the Sonora region of northern Mexico — the seasoning is subtle, but distinct rather than hot. Jerry Torres and family have owned and operated this eating place since its establishment in 1937. It is open every day except Monday, from 11:30 A.M. to 11:00 P.M., and until 1:30 A.M. Friday, Saturday, which are dance nights. The address is 233 West Mission Drive. Painting by Jake Lee.

Guacamole
4   avocados
3   green onions, finely minced
1/2 fresh tomato, finely chopped
1   sprig coriander, finely chopped
    (or pinch of powdered)
1/2 clove garlic, finely chopped
1   tablespoon salad oil

juice of 1/2 lemon
salt and pepper to taste
Mash avocados; add remaining ingredients and whip into a paste. Serve as a dip with corn chips, fresh vegetables or potato chips. If prepared in advance, refrigerate and leave avocado pit in bowl to retard darkening.

Villa Chartier, San Mateo

A modern luxury restaurant with every facility as well as a choice of several excellent dining rooms — one famous for roast beef, another for exotic foods from Hawaii and the East Indies — for those who only want to stop for a meal. It is at El Camino Real and 41st Avenue in San Mateo — take the Hillsdale turnoff from U S. Highway 101 to El Camino Real south. Open for lunch and dinner every day. Painting by Robert Collins.

Villa Chartier Tenderloin Tips Sauté Stroganoff

3 pounds tenderloin tips, julienne
2 ounces cooking oil
1 medium onion, sliced very fine
3 shallots, chopped
1 pound fresh mushrooms, sliced
1 cup Burgundy
3 cups Espagnole sauce (basic brown sauce)
1 cup sour cream
12-ounce package wild rice, cooked

Place 2 sauté pans over fire until well heated. Pour a small amount of cooking oil in each pan. Place beef tips in one pan and sauté until browned. Place onions and shallots in the other and sauté until half cooked; add mushrooms, sauté slightly, then pour in Burgundy and continue to simmer until liquid is reduced by half. Add brown sauce to tips and bring to a boil, now add wine-onion-mushroom mixture, bring to the side of the fire and stir in half of the sour cream. Serve in casserole with a generous portion of wild rice and a spoonful of sour cream on top of each portion.

Saddleback Inn, Santa Ana

Patterned after a historic hacienda and located in the shadow of the magnificent Saddleback Mountain for which it is named, the Inn creates a fascinating picture of Indian lore and the early Spanish California ranch tradition with its authentic decor and museum collection. It is on El Camino Real at the Santa Ana Freeway and First Street. Overnight and vacation facilities. Dining room open for lunch and dinner; coffee shop serves 24 hours. Bruce Gelker is the owner and manager. Painting by Rex Brandt.

Pollo con Chili

Have butcher bone six 1½-pound chickens from the back, leaving the leg bones intact (save bones). When finished, the chickens should resemble an envelope. Season the inside of the chickens with salt and pepper and spread thin slices of Monterey Jack cheese in a single layer over the breast area, then a layer of Ortega green chilis over the cheese. Shape a ball of Spanish rice with your hands, and place in the center of the green chilis. Fold the chickens from right to left over the rice and from left to right over the top of the first fold of chicken. Fold from front to back in such a manner as to form an envelope around the stuffing. For each chicken, dip a 1-inch-wide strip of brown paper 18 inches long into some cooking oil, and proceed to wrap each chicken so that it forms a ball with the two legs sticking up. Roast at 375° for 1 hour, basting chicken frequently with Mole Sauce (below).

Mole Sauce

Brown the chicken bones in a medium oven for 25 minutes with 2 medium-size onions, chopped and sautéed. Add: 1 tablespoon oregano, 1 teaspoon cumin, 2 teaspoons paprika, 2 large dried chili peppers, ½ teaspoon cinnamon and 2 teaspoons brown sugar. Stir well, then add 2 No. 2½ cans Las Palmas Chili Sauce (or other canned Mexican hot Sauce) and salt, to taste. Thicken with 1½ cups peanut butter. Strain and use some of the sauce to baste chicken. Serve chicken with remaining sauce on the side. Serves 10–12.

Copper Kettle, Aspen

This is a delightful dining room, aglow with candlelight and firelight. Dinner menu features an international cuisine, changing nightly. Open for dinner only; closed Sunday evening. Reservations necessary for dinner. Closed from October 1 to December 20, and from April 5 to June 10. Painting by Sara L. Uffelman.

Chocolate Torte, Lili

1 cup strong, cold coffee
1½ tablespoons sugar
2 tablespoons Grand Marnier (orange-flavored brandy)
½ pound sweet butter
2 large eggs
12 ounces semisweet chocolate, melted
40 vanilla wafers
1 cup whipping cream
candied cherries, angelica, colored sugar crystals, for garnish

Combine coffee with sugar and Grand Marnier. Cream butter, then beat in eggs and melted chocolate. Line a 2-pound bread pan with silver foil, allowing enough to hang over the edges to cover the top. Arrange a layer of vanilla wafers on bottom of pan. Sprinkle generously with the coffee liquid then spread with the chocolate cream. Continue in layers until the cream is used — ending with a layer of wafers. Fold foil over to cover top. Set an identical pan on top of the cake, weighted down with a heavy stone or can. Let season in refrigerator at least 12-16 hours, preferably 24. To serve, carefully remove foil. Turn out on serving platter. Frost top and sides with cream whipped and flavored lightly with Grand Marnier. Garnish sparingly with candied cherries, etc. Slice thin — it's really rich. Serves 12.

Toklat in Aspen, Aspen

Stuart and Isabel Mace own and operate this unusual restaurant which is right under Aspen Ski Lift Number 1, just three blocks south of Aspen's main street (State Highway 82). The building is constructed entirely of native log and stone; giant red spruce beams bridge the main dining room and give it an open comfortable feeling. Open daily during the winter season for breakfast, lunch and dinner; reservations preferred. Closed on Wednesday in the summer; also closed first of October to December 15, and April 14 to June 15. Painting by Clayton Staples.

Toklat's Alaskan Meatballs

Mix together: 1 pound choice lean ground beef; 1 pound choice ground lamb shoulder (or use moose or reindeer if you have it); 3 cups sourdough breadcrumbs; 1 cup chopped parsley; 1 cup chopped green onions; 4 cups chopped spinach, beet tops or Russian sourgrass; 2 large cloves garlic, mashed; 6 eggs; 1 cup coarsely grated sharp Cheddar cheese; 1 teaspoon salt and a good dash of coarse pepper. Mix ingredients well and form into golf-ball-size pieces. Brown meatballs in heavy skillet with ample oil over hot flame. Place in baking dish 2 layers deep. Sprinkle with $1/2$ cup each of chopped parsley and grated cheese and cover with about 2 cups tomato juice. Bake uncovered in 350° oven for 30-45 minutes, until bubbling. Serve at once. Serves 8–10.

The Ranchouse Restaurant, Estes Park

This unique loghouse restaurant is located on Highway 7, 1½ miles south of Estes Park. In a casual, relaxed atmosphere reminiscent of the Old West, delicious home-cooked food is served by attractive college girls who work here during their summer vacation. The restaurant is open only during the summer tourist season, seven days a week, from 7:00 A.M. until 9:00 P.M.; closed from October through May. Painting by William Deno.

Beef Stroganoff
1 pound beef tenderloin, sliced into 1½-inch strips
¼ cup green onions, chopped
¼ cup mushrooms, chopped
2 tablespoons butter
salt and pepper to taste
1½ cups brown gravy
¼ cup sour cream
¼ cup Burgundy
2 cups hot noodles

Sauté beef, onions, mushrooms, in skillet with butter until meat is a light brown. Add salt and pepper. Stir in gravy, and sour cream and stir often. Cook over low fire for 5 minutes. Add wine to suit individual taste. Serve over noodles in a casserole. Serves 4.

Ishii Garden, Honolulu

Guests leave their shoes outside, don a kimono and sit down on the floor to dine in true Japanese style in this restaurant. It is a typical Nipponese teahouse in a quaint rock garden setting where sukiyaki, at its best, is cooked at your table and served in Oriental fashion by kimono-clad attendants. Four private rooms and two cottages are on the grounds. A minimum group of four and a maximum of 250 can be served. Reservations necessary. Painting by Louis Pohl.

Sukiyaki

1½ pounds top sirloin in bacon-thin slices, 4 inches long
1 can sukiyaki-no-tomo (mushrooms, bamboo shoots, noodles)
½ pound green onions, cut lengthwise, 2 inches long
2 white onions, sliced lengthwise
4 stalks celery, cut diagonally, ½-inch pieces
Tofu (bean curd), 1-inch cubes, optional

Sauce

Combine ½ cup shoyu (soy sauce), ½ cup water, 2 tablespoons sake (rice wine), 4 tablespoons sugar.

Melt butter or suet in a large skillet and lightly sauté beef. Pour sukiyaki sauce over beef and bring to slight boil, then reduce heat. Add all other ingredients and cook 2 to 3 minutes. Do not stir vegetables while cooking but gently fold them under with large spoon about halfway through cooking time. If no large skillet is available, cook ½ recipe at a time. *Do not overcook.* Serves 4.

La Ronde, Honolulu

Perched atop the Ala Moana Building in the center of the shopping center of the same name, this dramatic dining room is at 1441 Kapiolani Boulevard. One of the first revolving restaurants, it offers a magnificent and changing view of Honolulu and surrounding areas. Lunch served 11:30 A.M. to 2:30 P.M.; dinner hours are 5:30 P.M. to 10:30 P.M. Sunday brunch is from noon to 3:00 P.M. Open seven days a week; reservations recommended. Painting by Dick Moore.

Stuffed Lobster Salad
5   cooked lobster tails
2   stalks celery, chopped
$^1/_4$ teaspoon salt, or to taste
pinch of pepper
juice of 1 lemon
$^1/_2$ cup mayonnaise
Remove lobster meat from shells and cut into bite-size pieces. Combine remaining ingredients except mayonnaise and mix well. Add mayonnaise a little at a time until you have desired consistency. Place salad mixture back in shells and serve on bed of lettuce garnished with lemon wedges. Serves 5.

Coco Palms, Wailua Beach

This Polynesian resort, one of Hawaii's most beautiful, is on the banks of a palm-fringed lagoon by the sea at Wailua Beach on the island of Kauai. Breakfast, lunch and dinner served daily until 10:00 P.M. Overnight accommodations and complete vacation facilities. Reservations necessary. Painting by Emil Major.

Potato Fromage

5 potatoes
10 potato shells, or 6 ramekins
3 tablespoons melted butter
¼ cup cheese sauce
2 egg yolks
salt and pepper to taste
¼ cup hot milk

Peel potatoes, quarter, and keep in cold water until ready to use. Place potatoes in saucepan with enough water to cover. Bring to boil, then re-duce heat. Continue cooking for 30 minutes. Remove potatoes from saucepan and beat with electric beater at low speed until well mashed. Add butter, cheese sauce, egg yolks, milk, salt and pepper. Continue to beat until light and fluffy. Place mashed potatoes in pastry bag and squeeze into empty potato shells or ramekins. Bake at 450° for 10 minutes until brown. Serves 6.

West

Colonial Inn, Blackfoot

Established in 1950 by the Charles O'Neal family, this restaurant is housed in a historic mansion built by the pioneer Kennedy family in the late 1800s. Dinner only served; closed on Monday. Reservations necessary on weekends and for Wednesday smorgasbord. It is just west of, and visible from, U.S. Highways 91 and 191. The address is 695 South Ash Street. Painting by Edwin Fulwider.

Celery Casserole
3   cups celery, diced
1/4 cup almonds, slivered
1/2 cup water chestnuts
5   tablespoons butter
3   tablespoons flour
1   cup chicken broth
3/4 cup half-and-half
1/2 cup mushrooms
1/2 cup Parmesan cheese
1/2 cup breadcrumbs
Parboil diced celery for 5 minutes.

Drain and put in casserole with almonds and water chestnuts. Heat 3 tablespoons butter and make smooth paste with flour. Slowly stir in broth and half-and-half. Simmer over slow fire for 5 minutes. Add mushrooms to sauce just before pouring over celery. Sprinkle with cheese, butter dots and breadcrumbs. Bake in 350° oven until bubbly. Serves 6. (This recipe can be used for green or lima beans as the main ingredient.)

Christiana Restaurant, Ketchum

Three blocks east of U.S. Highway 93 on Sun Valley Road, just a mile from the famed Sun Valley resort, this restaurant commands an excellent view of Mt. Baldy and the ski runs which come down from its 9,200-foot summit. Open for dinner every weekday; closed on Sunday and also during months of April and November. George Kneeland and Don Siegel are the owners. Painting by Don Bennett.

Carbonnade à la Flamande
3 pounds stew beef, cubed
2 tablespoons oil
salt and pepper to taste
dry light beer, to cover
1 level tablespoon of leaf thyme
3 bay leaves
1 teaspoon red wine vinegar
1/2 teaspoon prepared mustard

Brown 1-inch beef cubes in hot oil, then add salt and pepper to taste. Put in a tall casserole (4-6 1/2 quart) and cover beef with beer. Add thyme and bay leaves. Bring to simmer and cook about 45 minutes, or until meat is tender but not soft. Add vinegar and mustard. Mix well. Serves 6-8.

Golden Belle Restaurant, Billings

A fashionable dining room in the Northern Hotel in downtown Billings at First Avenue and Broadway, the restaurant is done in 1890s decor with old-fashioned chandeliers and wall coverings, and such decorative touches as a coffee mill from a pioneer mining camp. It is open daily from 7:00 A.M. to 11:00 P.M. during the winter; in summer months it opens at 6:00 A.M. Overnight accommodations. Painting by Lou MacMurray.

Butterfly Steak

14-ounce New York strip steak
3 tablespoons butter
2¹/₂ ounces House of Parliament sauce or A-1 sauce
1 teaspoon Grey Poupon mustard
2 drops Linghams English chili sauce
dash of monosodium glutamate and salt
2 grinds of whole pepper
2 tablespoons natural meat juice
1 ounce rum

Butterfly a 1-inch-thick steak (slice through center and flop open). Charcoal-grill to medium rare on one side. Place butter in pan over low heat, then add the steak, unbroiled side down, as soon as possible, to retain the heat of the meat. Start adding ingredients as listed, except rum, stirring rapidly after each addition. After sauce is made, add rum and flame, spooning the flaming mixture over the steak. When flame has gone out, place steak on serving plate and spoon remaining sauce over steak. Serves 1.

Gamers Confectionery, Butte

Founded in 1905, this restaurant is one of the oldest business concerns in the young state of Montana. A favorite with Gamers' customers for a half century is Cornish pasty, an Old World meat pie introduced to the area by early settlers — Cornish, Welsh, and Irish miners. A retail shop for baked goods and candy is operated next to the dining room at 15 West Park Street. Open 8:00 A.M. to 4:00 P.M. for breakfast and lunch every weekday; closed on Sunday. Painting by Elizabeth Lochrie.

Hot Cornish Pasty
Filling
1 pound sirloin tip
3 raw potatoes, cut fine
3 green onions, cut fine
salt and pepper to taste
Cut steak in small cubes, add vegetables and seasonings. Mix well.

Pastry
1 cup lard
1 ounce butter
4 cups flour
2 teaspoons salt
pinch of baking powder
1 egg
1 tablespoon cream

Cut shortenings into flour, which has been sifted with salt and baking powder, and add enough cold water to make a stiff dough. Roll out about $\frac{1}{8}$ inch thick and cut 6 circles about 6 inches in diameter — a saucer is a good guide. Into the center of each circle put a mound of filling ingredients. Moisten around the edge of the paste and press halves together at the edges with a fork. Brush each with a mixture of egg and cream beaten together. Make a hole in each to let steam escape. Bake at 425° for 1 hour. Serves 6.

Schell Restaurant and Townhouse Supper Club, Great Falls

Pastries, breads and breakfast rolls emerge from this restaurant's own bakery shop each day and are a favorite with patrons. At 306 and 310 Central Avenue in Great Falls, this establishment is open daily for breakfast, lunch and dinner. A luncheon smorgasbord is a regular feature. Painting by Bob Lindborg.

Stuffed Pork Chops
3 tablespoons butter
2 tablespoons onion, chopped
1 cup celery, chopped
1/2 teaspoon poultry seasoning
2 cups soft breadcrumbs
4 double pork chops, slit for stuffing
paprika

Melt butter, add onion, celery and poultry seasoning. Cook until soft and tender. Toss with breadcrumbs. Fill chops with dressing mixture. Sprinkle chops with paprika and bake in 350° oven about 45 minutes. Serve with country cream gravy. Serves 4.

Toasty Pecan Pie
Combine: 1 cup white corn syrup 1 cup packed brown sugar, 3 eggs, 1 teaspoon vanilla and 1/4 teaspoon salt. When mixed together, add 1 cup pecan halves. Pour into unbaked 2-inch pie shell. Bake in 350° oven for 50 minutes, or until done.

4 B's Cafe, Missoula

Open 24 hours a day, this excellent restaurant is at Bud Lake Village in Missoula. It is one of a chain of twelve 4 B's restaurants and cafeterias in Montana and Washington. Overnight accommodations at the Village Inn. Painting by Tom Palmerton.

Pork Teriyaki

3 pounds fresh pork, cut in cubes
6 tablespoons butter
2 cups turkey stock
1 teaspoon ginger
1/3 cup soy sauce
2 cups pineapple juice
1/2 cup brown sugar
2 tablespoons cornstarch
1 3/4 cups pineapple chunks
3 cups celery, chopped
1 1/2 large onions, chopped
3 1/3 cups bean sprouts
5 cups steamed rice
green pepper strips and carrot slices

Braise pork cubes in 3 tablespoons butter until well browned. Make sauce by heating together stock, ginger, soy sauce, pineapple juice and brown sugar. Heat well, then thicken slightly with moistened cornstarch. Simmer for a few minutes. Add pineapple chunks and braised meat. Braise celery, onions and bean sprouts together in remaining butter until just tender. Serve hot meat and sauce over steamed rice. Border with braised vegetables. Garnish with raw green pepper and carrot slices. Serves 8.

Louigi's Broiler & Italian Specialty Restaurant, near Las Vegas

For 16 years this friendly and informal restaurant has been popular for its fine food and excellent service. Four miles south of Las Vegas, it is at 3729 Las Vegas Boulevard (U.S. Highway 91 and 466). Open every day for dinner from 4:30 P.M. to 1:00 A.M. Italian dishes are the specialty of the chef, James Slife. Painting by Link Malmquist.

Chicken Cacciatore

Take two 2-pound fryers and disjoint wings, breasts, thighs and drumsticks. Sauté in olive oil for 25 minutes; Add: 1 teaspoon minced garlic; 1 medium onion, sliced; 2 large green peppers, sliced; 1 pound mushrooms, sliced; and 32 ounces canned tomatoes or 8 fresh tomatoes. Season with 1/4 teaspoon sweet basil, 1/4 teaspoon oregano, and salt and pepper to taste. Simmer for 30 minutes. Serve with spaghetti or steamed white rice. Makes 4 generous portions.

Veal Giovanni

Use four 3-ounce veal cutlets. Prepare a batter consisting of: 1 1/2 cups sour cream, 1 egg and 2 tablespoons red wine vinegar. Blend thoroughly. Marinate cutlets in batter for 1 hour. Combine 3 cups breadcrumbs with 1 tablespoon salt, 1 teaspoon pepper and 2 tablespoons minced parsley. Wipe excess sour-cream batter from cutlets, leaving a thin film on each. Coat with breadcrumb mixture and sauté in butter over medium heat until brown on both sides. Garnish with sautéed button mushrooms. Serves 4.

Eugene's, Reno

Only ten minutes south of the downtown hotels of Reno, this restful restaurant, surrounded by well-tended lawn and shade trees, is set back from U.S. Highway 395 (2935 Virginia Street). The interior is a blend of comfort and quiet elegance and the excellent Continental cuisine has a pronounced French accent. Dinner served 5:00 P.M. to 11:30 P.M. Closed Mondays. Reservations necessary for four or more. Painting by Link Malmquist.

Chicken Sauté Cynthia

Bone a 2½-pound chicken and cut into 4 pieces: 2 leg and 2 breast sections. Season and dredge in flour. Sauté without browning in butter until nearly done, about 20 minutes. Add 8 fresh mushrooms, ½ onion, finely sliced, and cook for 3 minutes more. Then add 1 cup dry champagne and 1 cup whipping cream and let simmer until reduced by about half, and then blend in 1 tablespoon Curaçao and the juice of ½ lemon. Place on a platter and surround with 20 seedless grapes and 10 orange quarters. Sprinkle with 1 tablespoon sliced truffles. Serves 2.

Tiffany's Restaurant, Cerrillos

On State Highway 10 midway between Santa Fe and Albuquerque, this 105-year-old former saloon is now an excellent restaurant in the ghost town of Cerrillos. On Sunday and holidays meals are served from noon to 8:00 P.M.; other days, dinner only served from 5:00 P.M. to 10:00 P.M. Closed on Monday and Tuesday. Open from April 1 to end of November. Painting by Louise B. Hansen.

Tiffany's Bean Pot Soup

2 cups dried pinto beans
1 pound ham, cubed
1 quart water
22-ounce can tomato juice
2 cups chicken stock
3 onions, chopped
3 cloves garlic, minced
3 tablespoons parsley, minced
¼ cup green pepper, chopped
2 tablespoons brown sugar
1 tablespoon chili powder
1 teaspoon each: salt, crushed bay leaves, monosodium gluta- mate and oregano
¼ teaspoon each: rosemary leaves, crushed, celery seed, ground thyme, ground marjoram and sweet basil
1 cup sherry

Cover beans with water and soak overnight. Add remaining ingredients, except sherry. Bring to a slow boil and simmer for 3 hours or until beans are tender. Add sherry. Serve in generous soup bowls, topped with chopped green onions. 6 generous servings.

The Ranch Kitchen, Gallup

Noted for its good home-style cooking and Western decor as well as its fine collection of Indian arts and crafts, this restaurant is about a mile and a quarter west of Gallup on U.S. Highway 66. Breakfast, lunch and dinner every weekday; not open for lunch on Sunday. Painting by Mark Storm.

Chili

1/2	cup corn oil
1	rounded tablespoon garlic, chopped
2 1/2	pounds hamburger
2	tablespoons freshly ground chili pepper
2 1/2	tablespoons ground cumin seed
3	teaspoons salt
1/2	teaspoon black pepper
3	cups condensed tomato soup
3	cups plain cooked pinto beans
3	cups water

Heat oil, add garlic and meat. Cook slowly until meat is done. Add chili, cumin, salt and pepper. Cook for 15 minutes. Add tomato soup, beans and water. Simmer until done. Serves 10.

Nut Bread

Cream together 2 tablespoons butter; 3 tablespoons vegetable shortening and 1 cup sugar. Then add 2 eggs, 3 tablespoons orange marmalade and 1 small cooked potato, mashed. To 4 1/2 cups sifted flour add 4 1/2 teaspoons baking powder, 1 teaspoon soda and 1 teaspoon salt. Sift flour alternately into batter with 2 cups orange juice. Slowly beat after each addition. Stir in 1 cup coarsely chopped pecans. Half-fill 2 or 3 greased loaf tins and bake covered in 350° oven for 20 minutes. Uncover and cook for 35 minutes. At the Ranch Kitchen the bread is sliced thin and toasted for breakfast.

The Bishop's Lodge, Santa Fe

This fine resort ranch, nestled in the foothills of the Sangre de Cristo Mountains, offers riding, swimming, golf, hiking, picnicking, skiing, and pack trips, in season. Lodge is open for breakfast, lunch and dinner every day year around; reservations necessary. It is three miles north of U.S. Highways 64, 84 and 285, on the north edge of Santa Fe, New Mexico, on Bishop's Lodge Road. Painting by Josef Bakos.

Bishop's Lodge Lacy Cookies
2   cups butter
1   cup white sugar
1   cup brown sugar (light or dark)
2   eggs, separated
1   teaspoon baking powder
2½ cups oatmeal, regular uncooked
1   teaspoon vanilla
1   cup walnuts, chopped

Cream butter, add both kinds of sugar and whip. Stir in egg yolks. Mix baking powder and oatmeal together and add to the mixture. Stir in vanilla and fold in nuts. Beat egg whites to form a stiff peak and fold into the batter. Drop by teaspoonfuls 3 inches apart on greased cooky sheet and bake approximately 8 minutes in a 300° oven. Cool 2 minutes and remove from cooky sheet. Yields 3 dozen.

Three Cities of Spain, Santa Fe

This restaurant is in a 200-year-old building that is considered one of the finest remaining U.S. territorial structures. Near the Indian Pueblos and a ski area, it is a popular spot for visitors the year around. Entertainment nightly during the summer, several times a week in winter. Open daily for lunch. No dinner served in winter on Monday, Tuesday and Wednesday evenings. Reservations advisable in the summer. The address is 724 Canyon Road, on the east side of Sante Fe. Painting by James Haughey.

Chili Verde Con Carne (Green Chili Stew)

Cut 2 pounds lean beef into 1-inch cubes and brown in 1 tablespoon hot oil or fat. Add: 1 teaspoon salt, 1 cup beef stock or hot water, 1 cup onion, chopped, 2 cups tomatoes; 1 can (1-pound 10-ounces) green chili strips, and 1 small garlic clove, chopped. Simmer until beef is tender, about 2 hours. Serve with pinto beans.

Cream Cheese Cake

Make graham-cracker crust right in a 10-inch springform pan by mixing: 1⅓ cups graham cracker crumbs, ⅓ cup sugar and ⅓ cup soft butter. Line the pan. For the filling, cut 1½ pounds soft cream cheese into small pieces. Add 1 teaspoon vanilla and 4 eggs, one at a time, beating well after each egg. Blend in 1 cup of sugar. Pour over crust and bake for 20 minutes in a 375° oven. Then add topping. For topping, blend together 2 cups sour cream, 1 tablespoon sugar and 1 teaspoon vanilla. Spread over cake and bake 5 minutes more. Cake will be soft when removed from oven. Chill 4 hours before serving.

Ardovino's, Sunland Park

Through the picture windows of this 1910 ranch house, guests gaze out on a pool, desert scene, mountains and Rio Grande Valley. This fine restaurant is open every weekday for dinner from 5:30 P.M. until 11:30 P.M. Closed on Sunday. The address is 4501 Anapara Road, Sunland Park (six miles from El Paso, Texas). Going west on 80-A, turn off at New Mexico 273, Anapara exit. Follow restaurant signs for one mile. Painting by Adele Bichan.

Veal Ardovino
1 pound veal, thinly sliced
2 eggs, beaten
1 teaspoon pepper
3 tablespoons grated Parmesan cheese
1 tablespoon parsley, chopped
4 ounces breadcrumbs
2 tablespoons shortening, for frying

Dip the sliced veal lightly in beaten eggs, then in crumbs combined with pepper, cheese, and parsley. Fry in hot shortening for a few minutes on each side, or until golden brown. Serve topped with sauce.

Sauce
Put ¼ teaspoon meat extract, 1 tablespoon butter, 8 ounces beef broth and ½ cup Marsala into a pan and bring to a boil. Pour over cutlets and serve immediately while steaming hot. Serves 6.

Scampi Ardovino
In a skillet heat 5 tablespoons butter. Sauté 4 cloves garlic until golden, then add juice from ½ lemon. Add 16 jumbo shrimp, cleaned and deveined, and cook for 5-8 minutes, or until tender. Serve immediately while piping hot. Pour remainder of butter over shrimp. Serves 4.

Village Green Motor Hotel, Cottage Grove

This motor hotel, set far back from Interstate 5, offers a variety of facilities for a family vacation right on the landscaped grounds. These facilities include swimming, a pitch-and-putt golf course, a bowling alley and a children's play area. Reservations necessary for overnight accommodations. Breakfast, lunch and dinner served daily until 2:00 A.M. Cottage Grove is south of Eugene. Painting by John Waddingham.

Lamb Chops Stroganoff

8   thick loin lamb chops, fat removed
salt and pepper to taste
flour
½   teaspoon mace
2   ounces butter
1   ounce brandy
2   small onions, sliced thin
bacon drippings
1   tomato, sliced thin
1   slice dill pickle, chopped fine
1   teaspoon lemon rind, grated
1   cup sour cream
2-3 ounces Madeira
4   cups steamed rice

Salt and pepper the lamb chops and dip in flour seasoned with mace. Brown on both sides in butter, add brandy and light. Sauté onions in bacon drippings and add to lamb chops, together with tomato, dill pickle and lemon rind. Over all of this pour sour cream mixed with the Madeira. Cover skillet and simmer over low fire until done: medium rare, 10 minutes, or well done, 15 minutes. Serve on steamed rice. Serves 8.

West

Surf Point Inn, Depoe Bay

The Pacific Ocean surf pounding against the rugged coastline is the view from motel units, apartments, and dining rooms at this imaginatively situated resort on U.S. 101, at Depoe Bay, about twelve miles north of Newport. Guests may swim in the ocean or heated pool, play golf, ride horseback, or fish. The dining room, open daily for breakfast, lunch, and dinner, features Polynesian and South Seas dishes as well as American food. Painting by Nelson Sandgren.

Chicken Aloha

1   3-pound frying chicken
1/2 cup onion, finely chopped
1/4 cup green pepper, finely chopped
2   cups tomato sauce
1   tablespoon Worcestershire sauce
1/3 cup vinegar
2 1/2 cups pineapple tidbits and syrup
1/4 cup brown sugar
1   teaspoon dry mustard
salt and pepper to taste

Cut chicken into serving pieces. Place in baking dish and cover with remaining ingredients combined into a sauce. Bake covered in 375° oven for 45 minutes or until chicken is tender. Remove cover about 15 minutes before chicken is done. Serves 4. (Sauce may also be used to baste baked spare ribs.)

The Pixie Kitchen, Lincoln City

In twelve years this restaurant has grown from a nine-stool counter to an attractive 200-seat restaurant. Excellent food is one reason for its growth; another is the establishment's imaginative way of welcoming children — there is an animated "Pixieland" to be seen from the dining room. Open for lunch and dinner daily. Reservations necessary during the summer and all weekends. Closed Christmas week. The address is 3519 Highway 101 (the Oregon Coast Highway) in Lincoln City. Painting by Emanuel Pitadakis.

Pixie Kitchen Clam Dip
8 ounces cream cheese
8 ounces minced clams
1 tablespoon mayonnaise
1/2 teaspoon garlic salt
1 tablespoon Worcestershire sauce
1/4 teaspoon monosodium glutamate
clam juice

Mix all the ingredients, adding clam juice for consistency desired, then refrigerate. The secret to the success of this dip is to make it at least 4-7 days before serving, which allows all the flavors to blend.

The Bluebird, Logan

For over a half-century this establishment has been in the restaurant and candy business in the center of Logan, which is nestled in the rugged Wasatch Mountains. Breakfast, lunch and dinner served daily; closed Thanksgiving and Christmas Day. The address is 19 North Main Street — U.S. Highways 91 and 89. Painting by V. Douglas Snow.

Tasty Egg Croquettes

2 tablespoons butter
2 tablespoons flour
³/₄ cup milk
¹/₂ teaspoon onion, minced fine
1¹/₂ teaspoons parsley, chopped
pinch of celery salt
salt and pepper to taste
7 hard-boiled eggs
1 cup flour
1 egg mixed with 1 cup milk
1 cup cracker crumbs
deep fat for frying

Melt 2 tablespoons butter in a skillet, then blend in 2 tablespoons flour. Cook over low heat, then add ³/₄ cup milk, the onion, parsley, celery salt and salt and pepper. Bring to light boil, remove and cool. Chop hard-boiled eggs in a mixing bowl, pour cooled sauce over them and mix well. Chill in refrigerator for about 2 hours. Then form into 8 croquettes, roll in flour, dip in mixture of 1 cup of milk and 1 egg, and finally roll in cracker crumbs. (Croquettes can be covered and kept in refrigerator for 2-3 days. Bring to room temperature before cooking.) Fry in deep fat for 5 minutes at 350° — or pan fry, keeping croquettes about 1¹/₂ inches thick, in 1 inch of cooking oil. Fry 3 minutes on each side. Delicious for breakfast or brunch. Serve plain or topped with creamed chipped beef or ham au gratin. Serves 8.

Balsam Embers, Salt Lake City

Boyd F. Summerhays is the chef as well as the owner and manager of this candlelighted dining room at 1450 Foothill Boulevard (U.S. Highway 40) southeast of Salt Lake City. Dinner served every weekday from 6:00 P.M. to 10:00 P.M.; reservations necessary. Closed on Sundays and holidays. Painting by Roy Kerswill.

Medallions of Veal Oscar

1½ pounds boneless veal, leg or rump
¼ cup all-purpose flour
¾ teaspoon salt
dash of pepper
12 ounces fresh crab legs, shelled
2 tablespoons all-purpose flour
1 well beaten egg
½ cup soft breadcrumbs
¼ cup butter or margarine
½ cup sauterne
1 cup Béarnaise Sauce

Cut veal into 9 pieces. Flatten with a mallet. Combine flour, salt and pepper; coat veal. Dip crabmeat in 2 tablespoons flour, then in beaten egg, and finally in breadcrumbs. Set aside. Fry veal in 2 tablespoons of the butter till golden brown. Remove to warm platter. Simmer sauterne in hot skillet for 1 minute and pour over veal. Place veal uncovered in a low oven to keep warm. In another skillet fry crab in remaining butter till brown. Remove from heat; keep warm. Place one heaping teaspoon Béarnaise Sauce over each piece of veal; top with crab. Pass additional sauce. Serves 4-6.

Cafe Paprika, Salt Lake City

The lighted candles on each table cast a soft light on the dining-room walls, which are lined with copies of old masters. German specialties are favorites on the Continental menu. Dinner served 6:00 P.M. to 10:00 P.M. daily. Closed Sunday. David Turner and Frank Hirase, owners, suggest weekend reservations. At the eastern entrance to Salt Lake City, this restaurant is at 2302 Parleys Way (Alt. 40). Painting by V. Douglas Snow.

Apple Strudel
4 cups apples, sliced
$^1/_2$ cup lemon juice
1 teaspoon cinnamon
1 teaspoon nutmeg
1 cup raisins
$^1/_2$ cup sugar
$^1/_2$ cup brown sugar

Crust
Mix by hand: 2 cups flour, 1 cup margarine, pinch of salt and pinch of sugar and enough ice water to make a firm dough. Roll crust and form oblong 7 to 8 inches long, 4 inches wide and 3 inches high at sides. Combine filling ingredients and pack into center of crust, then fold crust over the top. Cut two rows of small slits along the top. Bake at 350° until browned, about 45 minutes. When cooled, brush with sugar frosting (1 cup powdered sugar mixed with water until smooth). Serve with ice cream. Makes 8 portions.

Sky Room, Hotel Utah, Salt Lake City

Adjacent to famed Mormon Temple Square at South Temple and Main Streets in downtown Salt Lake City, this famous hotel, built in 1911, has combined modern convenience with the charm of the old. The Sky Room, on the top floor, is open for lunch and dinner daily, and reservations are requested. The hotel has several other dining rooms, as well as a motor lodge a few blocks away. Painting by Doug Snow.

Hotel Utah Borscht

To 1 quart of beet juice add 2 cups of chicken stock, 1 teaspoon salt, 1 teaspoon monosodium glutamate and 2 teaspoons fresh lemon juice. Bring to a boil. Dissolve 2 tablespoons cornstarch in a little cold water and add to hot liquid. Boil slowly for 5 minutes. Then combine 2 cups sour cream with 4 egg yolks; mix well. Beat this with 1 cup of the hot beet-juice mixture. Then add sour-cream mixture to soup. Bring to a boil, *but do not boil.*

Garnish with unsweetened whipped cream, chopped egg yolk and parsley. Serves 8.

French Toast

Slice a 9-inch loaf of white bread into slices approximately $1^1/_2$-inches thick. Soak slices in 9 beaten eggs for 15 minutes. Fry in butter on both sides until golden. Bake in oven for 10 minutes. Sprinkle with powdered sugar and lemon juice; glaze under broiler for a few seconds. Serves 6.

West

Aggie's, Port Angeles

A perfect vacation spot, this resort-motel at 535 East First Street, Port Angeles, provides good food and a wealth of recreation. Located on the Olympic Peninsula, close to fine trout and salmon fishing waters, the town is only a short distance from Olympic National Park, which is larger than the state of Rhode Island. The dining room is open every day 7:00 A.M. to 1:00 A.M. Overnight accommodations; closed only on Christmas Day. Painting by Harry Bonath.

Crab Louie
1   head lettuce
3   pounds crabmeat, fresh or frozen
2   cups mayonnaise
$^1/_2$ cup cocktail sauce
2   tablespoons Worcestershire sauce
$^1/_2$ cup milk
2   tablespoons vinegar
1   cup sweet pickle relish
1   large hard-boiled egg
1   thick slice of onion, grated
Optional garnish: crab legs, tomato wedges, olives, carrot curls, green pepper rings, lemon wedges, and parsley.

Before serving, place crisp whole lettuce leaves to form cups in chilled bowls. Shred lettuce to form bed of salad and place on top of leaves. Combine remaining ingredients, except crabmeat, and mix thoroughly. Add enough dressing to crabmeat to moisten, and place on top of lettuce. Spoon a little extra dressing over salads and add desired garnish. Makes 6 dinner-size portions. Serve with hot garlic bread.

Canlis', Seattle

Excellent food and service are the hallmarks of this distinctive restaurant, which is also notable for its contemporary Polynesian decor and its high, sweeping view of Lake Union and the city of Seattle. Located at 2576 Aurora Ave. North (U.S. Highway 99), in Seattle, Canlis' is open for dinner only 5:30 P.M. to 11:30 P.M.; closed Sundays, Thanksgiving and Christmas. Reservations advisable. Painting by James E. Peck.

Canlis' Shrimp
2   pounds prawns (giant shrimp)
2   ounces olive oil
$^1/_2$ teaspoon salt
$^1/_2$ teaspoon freshly ground black pepper
1   clove garlic
1   ounce dry vermouth
juice of 2 lemons
1   ounce butter
Shell raw prawns, split down the back and devein. Heat olive oil in a large skillet over a medium fire. Add shrimp and cook for about 4 minutes to a golden brown, turn shrimp over, add salt, pepper and garlic. Turn fire down low. When done, add vermouth, lemon juice and butter and cook for about 1 minute, stirring constantly. Serves 4 as an appetizer or makes $1^1/_2$ portions as a main course.

The Golden Lion, Seattle

Empress Josephine's carriage lamps mark the entrance to this elegant dining room in the Olympic Hotel on University Street between Fourth and Fifth Avenues in downtown Seattle. Here waiters garbed in East Indian costumes make a dramatic production of serving the 18 flaming entrees, served on swords or from chafing dishes, which are on the menu daily. Open every weekday for lunch and dinner; closed on Sunday. Reservations preferred. Painting by Rudolph Bundas.

Malayan Beef Tenderloin Tips

Heat chafing dish. Add $\frac{1}{2}$ cup butter and when sizzling hot add $2\frac{1}{2}$ pounds beef tenderloin tips cut into pieces 5x3x$\frac{1}{4}$ inch thick. Season to taste with salt, pepper and monosodium glutamate. Pour 6 ounces brandy over dish and flame off. Add 2-6 teaspoons curry powder, depending on how hot you want curry to be. Then add $1\frac{1}{2}$ teaspoons Maggi's seasoning, $1\frac{1}{2}$ teaspoons bottled steak sauce and 6 ounces Burgundy. In a separate pan blend together 6 tablespoons bottled curry sauce, 1 cup chicken stock and 2 cups whipping cream. Cook slowly to reduce and thicken and then blend into chafing-dish mixture. Sprinkle with a little sherry. Serve over hot-rice garnished with chutney. Serves 6 generously.

Ivar's Acres of Clams, Seattle

Situated on Pier 54, at the foot of Madison Street, facing the Seattle waterfront and bounded by schooners and fishing trawlers, this seafood restaurant invites the visitor to enjoy his meal on a flower-filled patio. For "dinner music" there are ferry whistles and ocean liners, outward bound. Lunch and dinner served every day. Ivar Haglund is the owner and manager. Painting by Harry Bonath.

Ivar's Poached Fish
4 half-pound pieces of fillet of salmon (or halibut or red snapper)
1 teaspoon allspice
1 bay leaf
2 onions, sliced
sprig of fresh dill or ½ teaspoon dill seed
salt to taste

Place fish fillets in salted water and simmer for 12 minutes. Add remaining ingredients to another pan of boiling water. Garnish fish with onion slices from the spice-filled pot. Serve with boiled potato. Ivar Haglund says this is a favorite recipe of real Puget Sound fishermen, a simple dish replete with natural juice and flavor. Serves 4.

The Space Needle, Seattle

Perched atop the towering symbol of Century 21, Seattle World's Fair, a spectacular revolving dining room 500 feet above the ground is reached by elevators at the tower base. While enjoying superb food, diners also view a magnificent panorama of the city, the Cascade Mountains and Puget Sound through the glare-proof glass walls that surround them. Open every day 10:00 A.M. to 2:00 A.M. Painting by James E. Peck.

Barbecued Salmon Scaloppine

For each serving cut 4 very thin slices through backbone of salmon — about 1½ ounces a slice. Marinate them for 2 hours in a good barbecue sauce and grill for 2 minutes on each side. Serve on top of rice pilaf with curry sauce.

Curry Sauce (for 12 portions barbecued salmon)

1 teaspoon butter
1 medium-size onion
1 medium-size apple
1 clove garlic
½ fresh tomato
2 teaspoons mild curry powder
salt to taste
½ medium-size banana
1 quart fish stock
½ teaspoon cornstarch
1 ounce dry white wine

Melt butter in saucepan, add onion, apple, garlic, and tomato, all chopped fine. Keep on medium fire for 10 minutes stirring frequently. Add curry powder, salt, banana, and fish stock. Cook for 1 hour and press through strainer. Bring to boil again and thicken with cornstarch diluted in wine.

Johnny's Dock, Tacoma

This excellent waterfront restaurant has an exciting view of the bustling activity of the docks and the ocean from its two-level dining room. From downtown Tacoma, cross the 11th Street Bridge and go for about 1½ miles; then turn left on Port of Tacoma Road and go to Pier 3 where the restaurant is located. Open daily 11:00 A.M. to 1:00 A.M.; Sunday 1:00 P.M. to 9:30 P.M. Closed Thanksgiving and Christmas Day. Reservations necessary. Painting by Robert Amundsen.

**Lamb Chops
in Sherried Orange Sauce**
4   shoulder lamb chops, cut at least ¾ inch thick
½   teaspoon salt
1   teaspoon monosodium glutamate
⅛   teaspoon medium-grind black pepper
2   teaspoons chicken-stock base
1   cup hot water
1   tablespoon currant jelly
¼   teaspoon grated orange peel
¼   teaspoon garlic powder
½   teaspoon bouquet garni for lamb
½   cup sherry

2   cups steamed rice

Brown chops thoroughly in a heavy frying pan. When brown, arrange chops in casserole or baking dish. Sprinkle with salt, monosodium glutamate and pepper. Pour off excess fat from base in hot water and add drippings in pan. Stir in jelly, orange peel and garlic powder. Simmer until jelly is dissolved. Crush bouquet garni and add, along with sherry. Pour over lamb chops. Cover and bake in 350° oven for 1 hour or until chops are tender. Serve with steamed rice, spooning the sauce over the rice and chops. Serves 4.

Inn at The Quay, Vancouver

Whether in the dining room or enjoying the comforts of an air conditioned luxury riverside motel room, patrons enjoy a magnificent view of the exciting Columbia River waterfront of Vancouver, Washington. This former port dock was converted to a dining and sleeping facility located at the foot of Columbia Street next to the busy Interstate Bridge. Open weekdays 7:00 A.M. to midnight; Sunday 8:00 A.M. to 9:00 P.M. Reservations suggested. Painting by John Waddingham.

Broiled Fillet of Columbia River Royal Chinook Salmon

Take six 8- to 10-ounce skinned and boned fillets of Columbia River Salmon and place in buttered shallow pan, baste with Savory Wine Butter and put under broiler until golden brown (approximately 8 minutes). Remove from broiler, garnish each fillet with Butter Crumbs, wedge of lemon and a sprig of parsley.

Savory Wine Butter

Melt $1/4$ pound butter, then stir in $1/8$ cup dry sauterne. Add $1/2$ teaspoon *fines herbes* (parsley, tarragon, chives and chervil, combined and chopped very fine) and a pinch of garlic salt.

Butter Crumbs

Take 3 slices dry bread and roll with rolling pin. Toast in oven until dry. Toss toasted crumbs with 1 tablespoon melted butter seasoned with salt, paprika and dash of lemon juice.

The Totem Pole Restaurant, Vancouver

Legend has it that almost a century ago pioneer travelers stopped for food at an old farmhouse on the site of this fine restaurant, located at 7720 Highway 99, two miles north of Vancouver, Washington. Today a combination of fine food and friendly atmosphere has made the Totem Pole (the name comes from the authentic Indian totem pole in the parking area) one of Washington's most popular family restaurants. Open for breakfast, lunch and dinner, from 6:00 A.M. to 12:30 A.M., seven days a week. Painting by John Waddingham.

Deep Dish Chehalem Blackberry Pie

3 cups Chehalem blackberries
2 cups sugar
1/4 teaspoon salt
4 tablespoons cornstarch
1 cup water
1 9-inch baked pastry crust
vanilla ice cream

Pour 3/4 cup water over 3 cups Chehalem blackberries and let stand at room temperature for 2 hours. Drain juice through colander into saucepan. Add sugar and salt and bring to boil. Immediately add cornstarch that has been dissolved in 1/4 cup water. Stir until dark and clear. Fold in uncooked blackberries gently. The secret is *not to cook berries.* Serve in individual deep dishes topped with piecrust and vanilla ice cream. May be warmed before service, but *do not cook.* Serves 6–8.

Canyon Cafeteria, Cody

In Buffalo Bill's home town of Cody, and at the east entrance to Yellowstone National Park, this attractive and modern cafeteria is popular with summer travelers who enjoy its fresh salads, homemade rolls and pastries. Open 5:30 A.M. to 8:30 P.M. every day during the summer season. Closed after Labor Day to June 1. It is on U.S. Highway 14 and 20 on the west side of the city. The management suggests that visitors to the area enjoy the Nite Rodeo, which is held in town every summer night except Sunday. Painting by Richard Brough.

Western Style Spaghetti and Meatballs

1¹/₂ pounds freshly ground beef
¹/₂ cup breadcrumbs
¹/₂ teaspoon salt
dash of pepper
2 tablespoons onions, minced
¹/₂ pound thin spaghetti
1 cup tomato juice

Mix thoroughly ground beef, crumbs, salt, pepper and onions. Make into 12 meatballs and brown in 375° oven for 15 minutes. Boil spaghetti in salted water until tender; drain and blanch in cold water. Then in a small baking pan arrange meatballs among alternate layers of spaghetti. Cover with well-seasoned tomato juice. Bake in 350° oven for 20 minutes. Serve piping hot with grated Parmesan cheese. Serves 6.

Pioneer Cafe, Jackson

Chef Joe Shockley and his wife, Mildred, are the owners of this restaurant, which serves good home cooking in a quiet and restful atmosphere. A mile east of U.S. Highways 187, 26 and 89, it is on East Broadway in the center of Jackson. Open daily 6:00 A.M. to 10:00 P.M., May 15 through October 15. Reservations necessary for large groups during the summer months. Painting by James Haughey.

Calf's Sweetbreads

1 pound calf's sweetbreads
juice of ¹/₂ lemon
4 tablespoons butter
4 chopped green onions
1 clove garlic, minced
4 tablespoons flour
2 cups beef stock
¹/₂ cup mushroom pieces
¹/₂ cup pale dry sherry

Drop sweetbreads in boiling salted water to which the juice of ¹/₂ lemon has been added. Simmer about 40 minutes or until tender. Wash well in cold water, separate from membrane, and slice or cut in chunks. Sauté green onions and minced garlic in butter. Blend in flour, slowly, then add beef stock to make sauce. Add sweetbreads, simmer about 15 minutes. Add mushrooms and sherry. Serve at once in a casserole. Serves 4. A green salad would complete this meal.

West

All-Time Favorite Recipes: 1946-1963

The all-time favorite recipes in this section have appeared previously in *Ford Times* and in one of the four volumes of *Ford Treasury of Favorite Recipes from Famous Restaurants* that preceded this edition. Each of these earlier volumes is now out of print and is a collector's item by virtue of the continuing demand. The following recipes are the ones our readers especially prized and have inquired about most often.

SOUPS

Jellied Cucumber Consommé
4 cups chopped cucumber
1 onion, sliced
1 tablespoon chopped parsley
1 teaspoon pickle spice
salt and pepper to taste
2 tablespoons gelatin
1 tablespoon lemon juice
sour cream
celery salt
paprika
Put cucumber in saucepan with 3 pints of water, onion, half of parsley and pickle spice. Bring to a boil and simmer 1 hour. Strain and season. Soak gelatin in 1/2 cup of cold water 5 minutes, then add to hot consommé. Cool, add lemon juice and pour into shallow pan. Chill in refrigerator until firm. Serve topped with sour cream, paprika, and rest of parsley. Serves 6.

Maine Fish Chowder
3 pounds haddock
6 slices salt pork
2 onions, diced
4 large potatoes, cubed
1 quart milk, scalded
1 teaspoon salt
1/8 teaspoon pepper
common crackers
Boil haddock and bone it. Fry salt pork and cook onions in the fat. Cook cubed potatoes in just enough salted water to cover. When potatoes are cooked, add salt pork, fat, onions, fish and scalded milk to potatoes and water. Salt and pepper to taste. Float crackers on chowder before serving.

Mom's Minestrone Soup
2 pounds pinto beans, soaked overnight
2 pounds fresh pork hocks, cut
1 large onion, cubed

1 cup celery, sliced
1 medium-size carrot, cubed
1/4 medium head cabbage, shredded
1 teaspoon rosemary
2 medium-size potatoes, cubed
2 tablespoons salt
1 teaspoon pepper
3/4 cup noodles
1 small onion, chopped very fine
1 clove garlic, chopped fine
3 ounces olive oil
Boil pinto beans in 8 quarts of water over low flame for 1 hour. Add pork and cook another hour. Then add all of the vegetables (except small onion and garlic) and the spices and cook slowly until vegetables are tender. Sauté onion and garlic in olive oil and add with noodles to soup about 15 minutes before serving. Serves 12–14.

Black Bean Soup, Princetonian
1/2 pound larding pork
1/2 Spanish onion, chopped
a few celery leaves
2 bay leaves
3 cloves garlic
1 1/2 cups flour
3 quarts water
1 1/2 pounds black beans, soaked overnight
6-8 potatoes, sliced
salt and pepper to taste
1 cup sherry
1 1/2 cups hard-boiled eggs, chopped
1 lemon, sliced very thin
Heat pork in heavy pan, then add onion, celery, bay leaves and garlic and fry for 5-8 minutes. Blend flour into mixture until it is smooth. Then add water and soaked beans. Bring to a boil and add potatoes to soup. Simmer uncovered for 3-4 hours. Remove from fire and strain through fine sieve. Season to taste and add sherry just before serving. Garnish individual bowls with chopped eggs and sliced lemon. Serves 10–12 portions.

MAIN DISHES

Round-up Stew
$2^1/_2$ pounds stew meat, diced
$^1/_2$ cup suet, diced
$^1/_2$ teaspoon pepper
4 teaspoons salt
1 teaspoon paprika
8 carrots, chopped
3 medium onions
6 spuds, cut small
4 stalks celery, chopped
$^1/_4$ small cabbage, shredded

Braise meat and suet in Dutch oven, add seasonings and water to cover. Cook 2 hours, add carrots, cook 15 minutes. Then add remaining vegetables, except cabbage; when other vegetables are almost cooked, add cabbage, cook for 10 minutes more, and serve. Water will evaporate, so check while cooking. Serves 6.

Kouzou Kzartma
4 lamb shanks
2 cups water
2 tomatoes, quartered
2 teaspoons salt
1 teaspoon paprika
4 large pieces potato

Wash lamb and soak in water for 15 minutes. Cook for $^1/_2$ hour at 375° in open roasting pan with tomatoes, salt, paprika and water. Turn meat over and cook another $^1/_2$ hour. Add potatoes and roast 30 minutes more, then turn the meat and potatoes and roast another $^1/_2$ hour. Serve with its own juice. This makes a complete meal for 4. Serves 4.

Brunswick Stew
1 6-pound chicken
2 cups lima beans
4 cups tomatoes
2 large onions, sliced
4 medium potatoes, diced
2 cups okra
4 cups corn
2 teaspoons salt
$^1/_2$ teaspoon pepper
1 teaspoon sugar

Cut chicken in 8 pieces and simmer $2^1/_4$ hours in 1 gallon water. Remove chicken. Add beans, tomatoes, onions, potatoes and okra to broth. Simmer until limas are tender, about an hour. Add hot water if necessary and stir to prevent scorching. Add corn and chicken, boned and diced, seasonings, and sugar. Cook till corn is done. Serves 8–10.

Intoxicated Loin of Pork
1 loin of pork for roasting
seasonings: 2 tablespoons salt, 1 tablespoon pepper, 1 teaspoon nutmeg, $^1/_2$ tablespoon sage, $^1/_2$ tablespoon marjoram
$^1/_4$ cup bacon fat
3 cloves garlic, cut
$^1/_2$ cup parsley, chopped
bouquet garni (1 large bay leaf, 1 sprig thyme, 2 sprigs green celery leaves, 1-inch horseradish root)
claret to cover
2 cups beef stock
flour

Rub pork well on all sides with the seasonings noted. Sear it in hot bacon fat containing cut cloves of garlic and chopped parsley. Put pork in baking pan. Add bouquet garni tied up with heavy white thread. Cover with claret and bake at 375°, allowing 30 to 35 minutes per pound. Turn the meat once in a while as it roasts. When the pork is done, the wine will have evaporated. Remove meat; pour in beef stock. Brown some flour and mix with little stock. Pour this roux into remaining stock and, stirring, heat to boiling. Season.

Schnitz un Knepp
3 pounds smoked ham, 8-ounce slices
4 cups dried apples
2 tablespoons brown sugar
2 cups flour
4 teaspoons baking powder
$^1/_4$ teaspoon pepper
1 teaspoon salt
1 egg, well beaten
$^1/_3$ cup milk
3 tablespoons butter, melted

Cover dried apples with water and soak overnight. In the morning cover ham with cold water and boil for 3 hours. Add the apples and water in which they have soaked and continue to boil for another hour. Add brown sugar. Make dumplings by sifting dry ingredients together 3 times. Stir in beaten egg, milk and shortening. Drop the batter by spoonfuls into the hot liquid with the ham and apples. Cover kettle tightly and cook dumplings 15 minutes. Serve piping hot. Serves 6.

Shrimp with Black Bean Sauce
1 tablespoon cooking fat
³/₄ teaspoon salt
1 tablespoon black bean sauce
1 pound shrimp, cleaned
piece of fresh ginger (size of green pea), minced
1¹/₂ cups sherry
¹/₂ cup stock
dash black pepper
¹/₃ teaspoon sugar
¹/₄ teaspoon monosodium glutamate
4 teaspoons cornstarch, mixed with ¹/₄ cup of water
4 green onions, chopped
Place fat in hot skillet, add salt, ginger and bean sauce. Stir in raw shrimp until sauce covers them. Pour in wine and stock and cover with tight lid. Boil 3 minutes. Add pepper, sugar, monosodium glutamate. Add cornstarch to make light gravy. Mix in onions. Serves 4.

Sole au Champagne
8 fillets of sole
soy sauce
1¹/₂ cups (approx.) champagne
salt and pepper
8 mushroom heads, peeled
6 egg yolks
1¹/₄ cups butter
2 tablespoons sour cream
Dip fillets in soy sauce. Heat enough champagne to cover the fillets. Add salt to taste. Poach fish and mushrooms 10 minutes. Remove to hot serving dish — flat oval is the best. Keep hot. Reduce cooking liquid quickly. Place egg yolks in a double boiler over hot, *not boiling*, water, add butter in small pieces. Then blend in cream, pepper and the reduced cooking liquid. Mix and beat well, with electric beater or wire whisk, until thick. The water must not boil. Correct seasonings. Pour sauce over fillets. Serves 4.

Enchilada Casserole
1 pound ground beef
2 tablespoons shortening
2 tablespoons chili powder
6 tablespoons flour
garlic, salt and pepper, to taste
1 quart water
12 corn tortillas
hot fat
1¹/₂ cups onion, chopped
1¹/₂ cups longhorn cheese, grated
Braise ground beef in shortening; add

chili, flour and other seasonings. Cook 5 more minutes, add water and bring to a boil. Cook 8-10 minutes. Dip tortillas in hot fat. Build up alternate layers of tortillas, onion, cheese and chili in an 8-inch-deep casserole. Heat in 375° oven for 20-25 minutes until bubbly. Serves 6.

Sour Cream Noodle Bake
Cook an 8-ounce package medium noodles in boiling salted water. Rinse and drain. Brown 1 pound ground beef in 1 tablespoon butter, then add 1 teaspoon salt, ¹/₈ teaspoon black pepper, ¹/₄ teaspoon garlic salt and 1 cup tomato sauce or puree. Simmer 5 minutes. Combine 1 cup chopped green onions, 1 cup sour cream, 1 cup creamed cottage cheese, and noodles. Alternate layers of noodle mixture and meat mixture in 2-quart casserole, beginning with noodles and ending with meat. Top with 1 cup shredded sharp Cheddar cheese. Bake at 350° in preheated oven 20-25 minutes, until cheese is brown. Serves 8.

Baked Halibut with Sauce
6 halibut steaks
³/₄ pound onions, sliced
¹/₂ pound mushrooms, sliced
2 No. 2¹/₂ cans tomatoes
1 cup tomato juice
1 clove garlic, minced
few sprigs parsley, minced
pinch of celery salt, nutmeg, Cayenne pepper and sweet basil
Sauté onions and mushrooms until soft. Add remaining ingredients, except fish. Simmer 30 minutes. Pour sauce in bottom of 6 casseroles. Place halibut on top of each. Cover with Cheese Sauce (below).
Cheese Sauce
Blend together 2 cups cottage cheese, ¹/₄ pound Parmesan cheese, grated; 3 egg yolks, ³/₄ cup very thick cream sauce and 1 tablespoon tomato puree. Place on top of halibut and bake 20-25 minutes in 350° oven. Serves 6.

Rock Cornish Game Hen Flambé au Cognac
6 1-pound Rock Cornish game hens
melted butter
salt, pepper and paprika
¹/₂ ounce brandy
Fill game hens with Dressing (below) and brush with melted butter. Sprinkle each

lightly with salt, pepper and paprika. Roast in 300° oven for about 1½ hours. Serve in chafing dish. Pour Cherry Sauce (also below) over hens just before serving. Pour brandy over sauce; light with match. Serves 6.

Dressing
Cook ¼ pound sausage, chopped, in a large skillet. Add 4 tablespoons water, 1 medium onion, chopped fine, and 3 mushrooms, sliced thin. Sauté until meat is well done. Add 1 cup cooked wild rice and season to taste with salt, pepper, poultry seasoning and 1 tablespoon brandy. Add ¼ cup bread crumbs and mix ingredients thoroughly.

Cherry Sauce
Combine 1 cup water, ¼ cup Burgundy, ¼ cup sugar and ¼ teaspoon salt. Bring to a boil and thicken slightly with cornstarch. Add 1 No. 2½ can black Bing cherries.

Chicken à la King
2 tablespoons butter
1 cup mushrooms, sliced
1 small green pepper, diced
2 tablespoons flour
2½ cups cooked chicken, diced
1 teaspoon salt
2 cups milk
1 egg yolk, beaten
1 pimiento, thin strips
¼ teaspoon black pepper
¾ cup dry sherry
1 cup chicken stock
8 French patty shells

Melt butter, add mushrooms and green pepper and sauté for about 5 minutes. Sprinkle with flour and blend it in. Add chicken and remaining ingredients except egg yolk and cook over low heat for about 20 minutes until sauce thickens; add egg yolk. Serve hot in patty shells. Serves 8.

Minced Veal à la Bernoise
¾ pound fresh veal
hot oil
1 tablespoon fresh butter
1 tablespoon onion, finely chopped
4 ounces fresh or canned mushrooms, sliced
1 ounce fresh cream
2 ounces dry white wine
salt and pepper and paprika to taste
parsley, to garnish
beurre manié (see below)

Cut veal in julienne strips and fry in hot oil for a few minutes until lightly browned. Drain oil and keep meat warm. Melt butter in saucepan and fry onions for 3 minutes. When onions are golden brown add mushrooms and veal. Mix well, add wine, salt, pepper and paprika to taste and cook for 3 minutes. Pour in cream and simmer for another few minutes, then thicken with 1 tablespoon *beurre manié,* pour in hot dish, sprinkle with parsley and a little paprika. Serve with hashed browned potatoes. Serves 2.

For *beurre manié,* combined 1½ teaspoons fresh soft butter with 1½ teaspoons white flour. Mix well together.

BREADS, MUFFINS, PANCAKES, COFFEECAKES

Swedish Rye Bread
2 cups dark rye flour
10 cups white flour
2½ cups lukewarm water
2 cakes compressed yeast
1 cup molasses
1 cup brown sugar
2 tablespoons salt

Mix all ingredients, knead and let rise overnight. Shape into 6 loaves and let rise double in bulk. Bake 45 minutes in a moderate oven. Each loaf will cut into about 10 slices.

Buñuelos
4 eggs
½ cup milk
¼ cup melted butter or margarine
3 cups sifted flour
1 tablespoon sugar
1 teaspoon salt
oil or shortening for deep frying
sugar
cinnamon

Beat eggs; add milk and melted butter. Sift flour, 1 tablespoon sugar, and salt into this and mix to make a soft dough easily handled without sticking. Make into walnut-size balls; roll on slightly floured board into a large circle like a tortilla or very thin pancake. Fry in deep fat until golden brown. Drain and sprinkle with sugar mixed with ground stick cinnamon. At Christmas serve Buñuelos broken into a soup bowl and covered with thin syrup made by boiling 2 cups brown sugar in 2 cups water flavored with 1 stick cinnamon and 1 whole clove.

French Pancakes à la Gelée

1/2 cup sifted all-purpose flour
1 egg
1 egg yolk
1/8 teaspoon salt
5 tablespoons milk (approximately)
3 tablespoons currant or red raspberry jelly
powdered sugar

Combine flour, egg, egg yolk, salt and milk. Beat with rotary beater until smooth. If necessary, add more milk to make batter the consistency of light cream. Cover; chill for 1/2 hour in refrigerator. Heat heavy iron skillet; wipe out with waxed paper which has been dipped in butter. Pour in enough batter to barely cover bottom of skillet, tipping while adding butter. Brown pancakes on both sides. Remove from skillet; spread with jelly; roll up jelly-roll fashion. Sprinke with a little powdered sugar. Place under broiler to glaze. Serve immediately. Yields 12 to 15 5-inch pancakes.

Orange-Date-Nut Bread

1 whole orange
6 ounces dates
2 tablespoons butter
1 egg
1 cup sugar
2 cups flour, sifted
1/2 teaspoon soda
1 teaspoon baking powder
3/4 teaspoon salt
3/4 cup nuts, chopped

Grind whole orange and dates. Strain juice from orange into a cup. Add hot water to it until there is 1 cup liquid. Add butter and 1 egg and set aside to cool. Put ground orange and dates in a bowl, stir in liquid mixture. Blend in dry ingredients, and add nuts. Pour into a well-greased 3 x 9-inch pan. Bake 1 hour in a 350° oven.

Christmas Stollen

1 cup milk
2 1/2 ounces yeast
5 cups flour
1/3 cup sugar
1 cup butter
pinch of salt
rum flavoring
1/2 cup almonds, chopped
1 1/2 cups raisins and currants, mixed
1/2 cup mixed fruit, diced (lemon and orange peel, citron and cherries)

Dissolve yeast in 1/2 cup lukewarm milk. Add 1 cup flour and mix to a soft sponge. Let stand about 1 hour in a room at 75°. Add remaining lukewarm milk, sugar, butter, salt, about 4 cups flour and rum flavoring. Mix to a fairly stiff dough. Add nuts and fruits; let dough rise about 1 1/2 hours. Make into 1 large stollen or 2 small ones, shaping like a Parkerhouse roll. Bake 45 minutes in 350° oven. When done, brush with melted butter and sprinkle with sugar.

Maple Nut Muffins

Sift together into a bowl 2 cups sifted all-purpose flour, 4 teaspoons baking powder and 1/2 teaspoon salt. Combine 1 egg, 1/2 cup milk, 1/2 cup maple syrup and 1/4 cup melted shortening, then add to dry ingredients, mixing until all flour is moistened. Stir in 1 cup chopped nuts. Fill 12 greased muffin tins 2/3 full and bake in 400° oven 18-20 minutes.

DESSERTS

Rich Lemon Pie

6 ounces sweet butter
1 cup sugar
juice and grated rind of 2 lemons
3 egg yolks (save whites)
1 whole egg
1 or 2 slices white bread
6 tablespoons sugar
8-inch pie shell, baked

Melt butter over very low heat; stir in sugar and lemon rind and juice. Beat yolks and whole egg together and add to mixture when sugar is dissolved. When thickened, remove from heat. *Don't allow to boil.* Remove crusts from bread and cut or tear gently into large crumbs and scatter over bottom of pie shell. Make a stiff meringue of the egg whites sweetened with 6 tablespoons sugar. While lemon mixture is still hot, spoon it over bread crumbs and cover with meringue. Seal meringue to edges of pie shell. Brown in 350° oven. Cool and serve at room temperature.

Walnut Pie

6 eggs, slightly beaten
1 cup white sugar
1/2 teaspoon salt

1 pint dark corn syrup
1½ teaspoons vanilla
2 cups walnut meats, chopped
10-inch pie shell, unbaked

Add ingredients in order listed and combine with whisk, but do not beat hard. Pour into pie shell and bake at 360° for about 1 hour, or until reasonably firm. Cool and serve with whipped cream or ice cream. Serves 10.

Pumpkin-Mince Pie
1 cup canned pumpkin
½ cup brown sugar
1 teaspoon pumpkin pie spice
½ teaspoon salt
2 eggs, slightly beaten
14½ ounces evaporated milk
2½ cups mincemeat
9-inch unbaked pie shell

Combine pumpkin, sugar, spice, salt, eggs and milk and beat until smooth. Spread mincemeat evenly over pie shell. Ladle pumpkin mixture carefully over mincemeat. Bake at 450° for 10 minutes, then at 350° about 45 minutes, until filling is firm in center.

Jefferson Davis Pie
½ cup butter
2 cups light-brown sugar
4 eggs, separated
2 tablespoons flour
1 teaspoon cinnamon
1 teaspoon freshly grated nutmeg
½ teaspoon allspice
1 cup cream
½ cup pecans, chopped
½ cup raisins
½ cup dates, chopped
10-inch pie shell

Cream butter and sugar together, then beat in egg yolks. Sift flour, cinnamon, nutmeg and allspice into mixture. Add cream, pecans, raisins and dates. Brown empty crust in 450° oven for 5 minutes; add filling. Bake in 300° oven until set, about 40 minutes. When cool, top with meringue made of egg whites. Brown meringue in 300° oven 15-20 minutes.

Lemon Velvet Ice Cream
Mix together 2 cups whipping cream, 2 cups milk and 2 cups sugar. Milk and cream should be very cold. Then add ⅓ cup fresh lemon juice, stirring slowly. Mixture thickens as juice is added. Place in 2-quart dasher-type ice cream freezer and freeze immediately to prevent curdling. Remove dasher before ice cream is completely frozen. Pack in salt and ice and let stand for an hour or more. For best flavor use the same day. This ice cream can also be made with good results in tray of electric refrigerator. Makes about 1½ quarts.

Gripsholm Apple Cake
4 cups tart apples, sliced
3 cups breadcrumbs
¾ cup butter
1 teaspoon cinnamon
1 cup sugar
pinch of salt
grated rind of ½ lemon

Peel and cut apples into thin slices. In a well-buttered baking dish arrange a layer of apple sections. Sprinkle with a mixture of sugar, cinnamon and crumbs. Add a few dots of butter to each layer. Fill dish with alternate layers of apple and crumb, with crumbs on top. Bake in 350° oven until apples are tender, about 45 minutes. Cool. Serve with Vanilla Sauce, whipped cream or ice cream. Makes 8 portions.

Vanilla Sauce
Mix together 1 cup milk, 1 cup light cream, 2 tablespoons sugar, ½ teaspoon vanilla and pinch of salt. Bring to a boil. Thicken over medium flame by slowly adding 4 egg yolks.

Marble Cake (1800)
Light Mixture
1½ cups sugar
½ cup butter
2½ cups flour
1 teaspoon cream of tartar
½ teaspoon soda
½ cup milk
4 eggs whites, beaten

Blend sugar and butter. Sift flour with cream of tartar and soda and add to sugar-butter mixture, alternating with the milk. Fold in egg whies.

Dark Mixture
1 cup brown sugar
½ cup each, molasses, butter
1½ cups flour
½ teaspoon soda
1 teaspoon cream of tartar
½ cup sour milk
4 egg yolks, beaten
pinch of cloves, cinnamon, nutmeg

Blend in same order as for light mixture.

Butter 2 bread-loaf pans and alternately spoon in light and dark mixtures. Bake in 350° oven for 1 hour.

Plantation Cookies
1/2 cup butter
1/2 cup brown sugar
1/2 cup white sugar
1 egg, beaten
1/4 teaspoon salt
1 1/2 cups flour, sifted
1/2 teaspoon soda
2 tablespoons hot water
1 7-ounce bar semisweet chocolate
1/2 cup pecan meats, chopped
1/2 teaspoon vanilla

Cream butter, add sugar and egg. Sift salt with flour, and dissolve soda in hot water. Mix these alternately with butter mixture. Add nuts and chocolate in small pieces. Flavor with vanilla and drop by teaspoonfuls on a greased cookie sheet. Bake 10-12 minutes in 375° oven. Makes about 4 dozen cookies.

Williamsburg Orange Wine Cake
1/2 cup butter
1 cup sugar
2 eggs, beaten
1 teaspoon vanilla
1 orange rind, grated
1 cup whole seedless raisins
1/2 cup English walnuts, chopped
2 cups sifted pastry flour
1 teaspoon soda, sifted
1/2 teaspoon salt, sifted
1 cup sour milk

Cream butter and 1 cup sugar. Add eggs, vanilla, rind, whole raisins and walnuts. Sift flour with soda and salt; add to mixture alternately with sour milk. Bake in greased square cake pan in moderate oven for 30 to 40 minutes.

Wine Icing
Mix 1/3 cup sweet, soft butter with 2 cups confectioners' sugar. Add sherry slowly, beating well. When desired consistency, spread on cooled cake.

Ozark Black Walnut Chocolate Torte
1/2 cup black walnuts, chopped
1/2 cup chocolate cooky crumbs
1 envelope plain gelatin
1/4 cup cold water
1 package semisweet chocolate
1/2 cup sugar
1/4 teaspoon salt
1/2 cup milk
3 eggs, separated
1 cup cream, whipped

Combine crumbs and nuts. Rinse out one 8-inch spring-form pan with cold water. Line with wax paper. Cover bottom with half of crumb mixture. Soften gelatin in water. Cook chocolate, 1/4 cup sugar, salt and milk in a double boiler until blended. Beat egg yolks and add hot mixture slowly, stirring rapidly. Return to double boiler; cook, stirring, till thickened. Remove; add gelatin, stir until dissolved. Chill until nearly thickened. Beat egg whites and add 1/4 cup sugar. Fold in chocolate mixture and cream. Turn into pan. Top with remaining crumb mixture. Chill till firm.

Ice Cream Praline
1 pint heavy cream
6 ounces granulated sugar
8 egg yolks
8 ounces praline paste
1 pint whipped cream
fresh strawberries

Mix cream with the sugar and egg yolks; stir while cooking. Remove from fire before mixture boils, and cool. Then add praline paste, previously prepared by cooking together to the caramel point equal quantities of almonds and sugar, which have then been cooled and reduced to a paste. Strain the mixture; add whipped cream and set in a paper-collared mold and freeze for 1 1/2 hours. Remove paper, unmold and serve, garnished with very ripe fresh strawberries which have been macerated in good orange liqueur.

Peach Ice Cream
1 heaping 2-quart basket peaches
5 1/2 cups sugar
1/2 teaspoon salt
1/3 cup lemon juice
3 1/2 quarts heavy cream

Peel and pit peaches, then grind. Add sugar, salt, lemon juice and cream. Freeze as you would regular ice cream. If your family is small, halve the recipe but don't underestimate anyone's capacity for this delicious summer treat.

RECIPE INDEX